Rocking Around the Clock

Rocking Around the Clock

Steffany Barton, RN

gatekeeper press
Tampa, Florida

ROCKING AROUND THE CLOCK

Published by Gatekeeper Press
7853 Gunn Hwy, Suite 209
Tampa, FL 33626
www.GatekeeperPress.com

Copyright © 2023 by Steffany Barton, RN

All rights reserved. Neither this book, nor any parts within it may be sold or reproduced in any form or by any electronic or mechanical means, including information storage and retrieval systems, without permission in writing from the author. The only exception is by a reviewer, who may quote short excerpts in a review.

ISBN (paperback): 9781662930331

This book is dedicated to Sue, my student and friend.
Nicole, my research assistant.
Victoria, fellow author and personal muse.
AJ, my north star

AUTHOR'S NOTE

I began this book during the pandemic, in March of 2020. At the time, I felt exuberant in sharing the information and inspired with the format. I expected myself to have the book done and released in a few months' time.

Of course, research took a while. Combing through stone candidates took some time. The biggest and meanest delay, however, came from within me. The closer I came to finishing the book, the more I doubted, criticized, questioned myself.

My soul sincerely longed to share the material. My angels and spirit guides patiently coaxed me onward. I wanted to give up. But I did not. I kept going.

Two and a half years have passed. I could have abandoned ship, tossed in the towel, waved the white flag of surrender to my insecure ego. I did not. I kept going.

I share this with you to encourage you toward your dreams. Rocks aren't formed in a day. Books don't write themselves. Dreams don't magically happen.

With time, tenacity, and determination, you will achieve and accomplish your soul's work. You can only succeed.

I believe in you. I send love to you!

Betty was my first love.

One day, as I contentedly explored along the banks of our creek, I noticed her. The afternoon sun played on the water painting ripples of light and dark as the wind ruffled the feathers of the cottonwood tree. Across the way and into the heavily forested area, I overheard the melancholy drone of a mourning dove. The clouds, stuffed and fluffed, floated lazily overhead. Conditions were right. Woodland magic was in the air.

She caught my eye. Unassuming but strong, simple but beautiful, she sat patiently waiting for me. I carefully bent down and gently picked her up. She fit snugly, warmly into my hand.

Betty was my first pet rock.

Reddish brown, smooth and bumpy, she was coated in a bit of clumpy dirt. I brushed her off carefully, knowing I had discovered treasure. Not a diamond, ruby, or pearl; she was Betty, my rock. Over the next few years, she became not just a material object, she was an anchor for my heart when I felt troubled. She was, in every sense, my rock.

As I scooped her from the earthen bed, I mentally compiled a list of the supplies she would need: I could use a washcloth as a blanket, and a tooth pillow as a bed (I never bought in to the Tooth Fairy business anyway). I'd set her on my books when reading, and she could go in my pocket to school. It was settled. I knew we would be fine together.

Back home, I burst through the door and excitedly announced to my mom, "Look, I found a pet rock!"

She stopped her meal preparation duties and met me with a smile. "Wow, I like this rock. Did it come from the creek? It has some cute bumps there!" she said.

"Yes, it was right there. I like this rock better than the stones and fossils I've found, better than the shells from Galveston. I think I will keep it," I must have looked silly, knees muddy, hair mussed, grinning widely with my buck teeth and freckles. Silly and happy.

Keep Betty I did.

That little rock started what has become a lifelong love of stones, crystals, and gems. I appreciate each natural treasure for its unique, quirky, raw beauty. No two stones are ever the same; nor should they be. Stones, trees, flowers, you, and me all have a wonderful, irreplaceable essence contained in our physical presence. All life embodies heaven on earth; it's our birthright and our highest destiny.

Through my teen years and in my early 20s, rocks became more of an accessory. I loved my turquoise earrings with my brown boots. I prized a lovely moonstone ring that looked perfectly out of this world with a pink shirt. A bracelet here, a necklace there, piece by piece, I curated a humble collection for wear. Stones became objects as I learned to produce and function at full speed in the world. Betty was out of my sight and no longer in my mind.

As a fledgling young adult, my world was rocked when my mom died. She left me, and her silver-plated mother's birthstone ring, behind. A few months after her funeral, missing her terribly, I mustered the courage to slip on the treasure, It fit perfectly even though her fingers had always seemed shorter and thicker than mine. This struck me as odd, but there was something more.

With the ring placed, I suddenly felt a sensation. Subtle, yes, and powerful, too. I had something physical to hold, something tangible in reach that drew me close to her. My heart beat faster as I took a sharp breath of hope. Something to anchor me in grief's storm.

Snapping quickly back to my senses, I took off the ring, thinking whatever had just happened was low blood sugar, too much caffeine, or just my ridiculous mind playing tricks on me. In that instant, I felt fresh anger at her loss, intense frustration that she died, rising up like steaming lava. I tossed the ring aside.

Several weeks later, I remembered her ring. Not that I had ever forgotten it, but I decided to think about maybe trying it on again. I must admit the prospect was bittersweet. I felt so happy that the ring fit, but so unhappy that she wasn't wearing it. I loved that I had it; I hated that she was gone. I sat on my bed and cried instead of getting the ring. Maybe another time…

And so once again, as happened with Betty, I forgot about the ring. Life rushed on, and I left my treasures behind. I have noticed that when I put myself in overdrive, the very things I fear are the ones that can heal me, help me the most. I worked hard at doing and even harder at not feeling. I convinced myself this helped me "heal," or at least avoid, the pain inside. Wearing the ring could have comforted me, working with stones could have soothed me. But it was simply not time.

One afternoon, nearly 15 years after my mom passed, on a whim, or perhaps by destiny, I opted to sort through my jewelry. Six months pregnant with my first child, I chalked it up to nesting urges. Looking back, I know this was something more than mothering instincts. My soul was quickening with renewed life.

Before I became pregnant, I started dabbling and dipping, experimenting and exploring in the spiritual side of life. From angels to oracles to Reiki, I whetted my appetite with all that was woo-woo. I practiced seeing auras, talking to Archangels, communicating with the deceased, and yes, working a bit with crystals and stones. My career as a nurse, though successful and financially beneficial, had left me feeling flat. When I opened to the unseen, I saw a glorious path where I could share and help others find a deeper meaning in life. I had found my way home.

I surprised myself with this interest. I had always prided my highly practical, well grounded, normal mindset. Even more surprising to me was the invisible world of spirit seemed tangible in my physical life. As it just so happened, I could see auras, I enjoyed conversing with Archangels, and I had a knack for hearing the voices of the dead. Strange but true; I didn't expect or ask for it, but it was there. I felt like

Dorothy when Glenda the Good Witch proclaimed, "You've always had the power my dear. You've had it all along." I stopped fighting and judging myself. I dropped the resistance against what felt so pure. Love is Love, I decided. I wanted to love, to be love.

That desire, that sincere and earnest longing to experience love, was the greater force at work the day I began sorting my armoire. Broken watches, unopened boxes, ugly broaches, earrings without mates, a few miniature teacups (where did those come from?), a seashell or two, and a ring. The ring. Sifting through the contents, I found a treasure lost.

Without hesitation I put it on. A flash of light and a wave of heat ignited within me and swept through me. I felt connected and protected. I felt inspired and calm. I felt the clear presence of my mom and my unborn daughter with me, cheering me on.

The ring had an emerald, ruby, and a light blue periwinkle set in silver. As I admired each stone, shifting my hands in patches of light, I was struck by the depth and richness of each color. I could feel strength pulsing as the emerald, joy giggling as the ruby, melody rising as the periwinkle. The stones were not just objects, they were beautiful containers of spiritual intelligence and ancient wisdom. Just like you and your body are.

So, I was hooked. Or re-hooked. My appetite for stones grew voraciously, and I have been learning as much as I can since then. Each stone tells a story, offers a gift, and sends a blessing. Every rock remembers its place, sees without judging, loves without condition. We can learn so much from seemingly inert, inanimate objects when we are willing to ponder the wonders of our world.

As I worked more methodically with stones, I found myself enthusiastically giving away and suggesting them to friends. Need a boost? Try some poppy jasper. Eyes fatigued? Try this iolite. Tummy trouble? Here's a bit of citrine.

Crystals work by the principle of coherence. The physical and mineral structure of a quartz crystal, whether mined in Colorado or Congo, will be the same. A ruby from South Africa or South Carolina will appear identical. The weather can change, the matrix of the stone remains. Yell at the stone, hide it in your closet for a decade or two, toss it out the window, whatever you do, the stone will remain atomically sound and molecularly consistent.

Unlike stones and crystals, our cellular structure changes moment to moment, day to day. Blood cells are broken down and recycled. Skin sloughs. Gravity tugs us down and our collagen thins; we age and wrinkle. Someone snaps at us, we feel hurt, cast aside and our cells start to change. Our bodies are affected by all that happens over, under, around, and through us.

As we experience these fluxes and shifts, we may struggle to find center. Maybe you've said a prayer a thousand times, but you still experience loneliness no matter how hard you try. Or, perhaps, despite every effort, a sense of peace seems to run and hide.

That's when crystals and stones can bless us beyond belief. Like a master tuning an instrument whose voice has fallen flat, crystals will reattune thoughts, emotions, and perceptions to a coherent, resonate, healthy point of view. Amazing AND true.

When feelings quiver and quake, tiger's eye can help you go with the flow setting emotions on an even keel. Amethyst sings in a true and pure voice a gentle lullaby of Love. Angelite awakens and attunes our essence to know angels. Simple physics helps us grow the complex metaphysical aspects of our selves. As we delve more deeply into the core of who we are, we express ourselves more truly in all we do.

Crystals are more than just trinkets; each stone is a story millions of years in the making. For example, in the 1800's a British prospector scoured the far, desert reaches of Nambia in search of gold. Sifting through the sands of time, he discovered a unique specimen, what is now called pietersite. This incredible mineral is a marbly mix of white, blue, and brown and looks like an "oasis" is the storms. The appearance compliments the therapeutic properties of pietersite; this crystal helps us see the light in the darkness and fortifies our heart with the strength to endure life's gales, winds, and difficult conditions. Those character qualities are more precious than gold.

Take ocean jasper, which was discovered by chance on the island of Madagascar one day when the tide was low. The earth revealed this spectacular specimen in a wondrous way, and it can only be collected during favorable conditions.

Moldavite is another amazing stone. Known as a tektite, this is the fusion of a meteor and the impact material on the ground in Czech Republic that was formed 15 million years ago. In the truest sense, this rock is heaven and earth.

Fulgurite is a formation left when lightning strikes the ground. In a flash of pure energy, for a split second, temperatures blaze hotter than the sun. As the site cools, the melted earth rapidly forges a hardened rock of distinct form. Holding this, we embrace the energy of lightning.

Earth gifts us with incredible crystalline treasure, millions of years in the making that can enliven us with tremendous power, peace, wisdom, and strength accessible now.

Just hold a rock.

As you're starting, remember that crystals are individuals and, as such, have unique effects. Some crystals work quietly in the background---but they still work. Some crystals come on strong then ease up until you forget they are there—but they still work. Some crystals may be just too intense—but they still work. Understand you may not "feel" the effect of some crystals immediately or even in several weeks' time. Don't give up! They work, even when you don't notice a huge change of heart or mind.

I think of crystals like perfume. Sometimes when you pick up a stone you may feel a strong and immediate sensation, like gussying up with loads of sweet-smelling perfume. After a while, you won't notice the crystals, just as you neglect to detect your scent. As we acclimate to an experience, our senses entrain to a new set point.

Some stones work quickly to bust an energy move. Purples, blues, and tektites are a few examples of fast-moving, strong acting, getting jiggy kind of crystals. Pink, greens, and some yellow gems are gentler but still create a buzz around your energy field. Oranges, reds, blacks, and browns are slow and steady but will always win the race. Working with a variety of stones from each of the colors will bring a rainbow of healing energy to your life. You'll feel strong, bright, and ready to take life on.

Often, friends or acquaintances will notice shifts in your energy before you do, commenting you seem "different" somehow. Maybe they think it's your hair, or perhaps you've lost a bit of weight or……

The truth is crystals change you for good!

The most important key to harnessing the power of stones is consistency. Your stones will work regardless of what you believe, how you feel, or where on the spiritual journey you may be. Let the stones sit near you, let them delight you, let them work for you. Our world is filled with magic, packed with endless treasure. Members of the mineral kingdom stand steadfast and true among these gifts. Allow them to comfort, inspire, energize, and delight you.

The size of the stone doesn't matter. Admittedly, I like big chunks and hunky pieces, but my wallet does not. When selecting stones, look for a size that feels

Goldilocks…just right. I encourage you to trust your intuition when purchasing or choosing. Your soul knows what you need; it can only help you.

Your stones, like you, will need a bit of good hygiene. My preferred method is to leave them out in the full moon. Sometimes I leave myself out in the full moon, too. Moonlight is transformative, helping crystals slough dust and debris.

Sage and incense easily clear your stones. Simply let the smoke bathe the crystals for a moment or two. Then bathe yourself in the cloud of sage. The smell intoxicates and the smoke cleanses. Take a few moments to enjoy the sensations. These small ceremonies, simple acts of recognizing the sacred in seemingly ordinary life, bring mindfulness and a deeper sense of connection to our heart and soul.

Some stones will lose color in direct sunlight. These include amethyst, citrine, fluorite, opal, rose quartz, turquoise, aquamarine, celestite, sapphire, kunzite, topaz, and smoky quartz. In my personal work with stones, I hesitate to place them in the sun. Crystals grow within the Earth and most are exposed to little or no sunshine at all. Imagine being jolted awake from a lovely slumber with beaming hot, intense light. Ouch! You might get your day off to a rocky start, no pun intended. Small increments of soft light for a short bit will cleanse your stones nicely.

The frequency of clearing is up to you. I recommend at least once a month. Your stones will thank you.

After you've chosen and cleared your stones, you're ready to get hands on—around the clock. As your energy waxes and wanes, ebbs and flows throughout the day, you'll have an hour by hour stone companion waiting at your side to optimize, balance, and support you. From dawn to dusk and all night long, you will be protected and nurtured by a beautiful assortment of healing gemstones. You can pop them in your pocket, set them out in a line, tuck them under your pillow, create lovely arrangements to soothe your body and mind. I will share with you a stone for each hour of your day, and you can choose how you carry, display, and access them.

If you have to travel and don't want to tote along an army of stones, I recommend taking a few of your favorites and then clicking a picture of the rest. If you need to connect, you have an image of your stones. This could be the wallpaper in your phone, your contact picture, or a loved image in your gallery. Having the essence of your stones with you will keep you grounded, even in the skies!

As you work through the list, please remember that this is not supposed to be a highly regimented, mechanical practice. These are stones, not London Guards at Buckingham Palace methodically, precisely rotating in and out at exact time. The hour-by-hour guide is a mindful way of utilizing a spiritual tool in your everyday life. When you are checking your energy, you can make clear decisions toward your good. Stones can enhance self-awareness, centering you as you go.

Please feel free to modulate the schedule for your routine. If you wake at 10am, use the first stone, pyrite, as your wake-up call. If you oversleep one day, the same guiding principle applies. Match the scheduled stones to your personal daily routine. Let this work with you and for you—all the time.

Because the weekends are different, I have cultivated a side garden of stones. The traditional weekend may be Saturday and Sunday, but if your days off are Tuesday and Thursday, use the weekend crew then. If you work four days on and three off, you'll use the weekend stones on your three off days. The stones chosen will enhance your ability to focus on work and enjoy your play.

For each stone, I will share how it enhances your energy field, the benefits you'll notice, and an affirmation for you to use. This provides a well-rounded, richly grounded approach to working with crystals. I know you'll be amazed at how gently and powerfully these allies will work for you.

Of course, stones are lovely and powerful, but you are ultimately responsible for your choices in life. Carrying a crystal won't magically melt away the pounds or cause a new car to spontaneously appear in the driveway. If you utilize a stone for health benefits, please remember to compliment that with traditional and medical therapies.

Years ago, I had an acquaintance who posted something very unkind directed toward me on Facebook. When I lovingly approached her, she immediately shot back that it was a crystal's fault. She claimed that a new stone she was wearing caused her to get angry and dizzy, and she couldn't stop the post.

Sounds ridiculous, right? Strange but true.

Being mindful of our choices, thoughtful with our words, and clear in our actions is our divine responsibility with or without the loving presence of mineral kingdom ambassadors. Stones don't do the work for you, but they can make the work a bit easier, more joyful as Spirit works through you.

Before we rock, I want to give you a peek inside to see the gears that will keep you turning and hands that can keep you moving. Let's go!

INNER WORKINGS

CHAKRA TIME

Energy. Chi. Vibes. Universe.

Whatever you call it, everything we see and anything we don't is comprised of energy. Through divine intelligence and creative wisdom, energy manifests in cohesive ways to inspire and teach us as we learn and grow.

Without a processing system, our energy colliding and crashing with the energy of the world would render us helpless. To prevent such chaos, we have evolved and adapted an array of energy powerhouses that facilitate our physical and spiritual navigation through the seen and unseen world.

THE CHAKRAS

Chakra comes from the Sanskrit word meaning "wheel of light." This descriptive term captures the appearance of our energy transformers when viewed from the front of the body. Picture looking at a tornado or whirlpool from above, and you will have a rough visual of these light wheels.

In an ideal state, each chakra exists in proportion to the others. Some are large, others small, yet all are designed in scale with one another. Each chakra can take in and process any energy; sometimes we like to put the concept in a box and think one chakra only handles one kind of energy, but this in not quite true. All the chakra translate energy according to a specific focus; when an impulse comes to us, we experience it holistically and globally.

Say you walk into the kitchen and smell cookies, ooey-gooey chocolate chip manna baking with lovin' in the oven. All of you begins to assess and process the situation. You will have physical responses through each of your senses. You may feel an emotional response. Your mind knows to call these little babies chocolate chip cookies, and you picture how these tasty nuggets look. You may ask when they will be ready or express some sort of anticipation. Perhaps you recall the past when your grandma had treats waiting for you at each visit; you may also realize that next week you're supposed to bring snacks to a work party. The past, present, and future you commune with the cookies. And you've not even dug in!

This is how our energy works. We are multifaceted, multidimensional beings swimming through an endless sea of energy.

To make our experience on Earth a bit more navigable, our energy body evolved differentiation. Just as similar cells bind together to make tissues which come together to make organs, our chakras have developed areas of expertise. The seven major chakras are as follows:

ROOT CHAKRA

Food, clothing, and shelter. Welcome to the base, or root chakra.

This area of our energy field tethers us to the Earth. Downward facing, the root chakra opens in the lower pelvis and includes the legs, feet, kidneys, and adrenal glands. Because this is our survival center, our finances, career, car, body, and family energy heavily influence this center. The color association is red.

When the root chakra is balanced, we recognize that there are more than enough resources for everyone, we allow ourselves to work at a measured pace, and place self-care as a priority. We eat when hungry, stop when full; sleep when tired and wake rested well.

We enjoy our home, find it comfortable and safe, and appreciate clean air and water. We feel content with having a physical body and at peace with who we are.

But, when we begin to resent our bodies, worry about money, ignore our inner cues, compromise self-care, or put others ahead of ourselves, we quickly wiggle and wobble around our root. With mild imbalances or disconnections from this energy center, we may feel spacey, experience digestive issues, become forgetful, or struggle with a lack of motivation. Quick and reliable indicators of root chakra issues are irritation and a feeling that something is "off." If the imbalance becomes more severe, we might experience depression, apathy, anger, anxiety, bone and joint pain, and resentment toward life.

The color of the root chakra is red.

Fortunately, Earth sculpts many offerings to assist in keeping our root chakra balanced, stable, and clear.

Generally, blacks, reds, and mahogany tones prove useful allies. Members of the chalcedony, jasper, agate, obsidian, calcite, and fluorite families radiate strong, steady energy that resonates with first chakra energy.

SACRAL CHAKRA

Tell me what you like and how you feel?

These are the focal points of our second energy portal, the sacral chakra. Shining forward and back from the body, this center is anchored in the pelvic bowl and specializes in how we sense and feel our way through life, and what we create along the way. Our desires, emotions, tastes, preferences, preverbal memories, and body image move through here. Physically, the reproductive organs, our blood, muscles, and body fluids correspond with the sacral chakra.

When balanced, we feel happy and content with life. Though storms and challenges may arise, we find buoyancy and allow our emotions to flow as they will. We appreciate regular cycles and seasons and embrace the sensual side of life. We reflect on and learn from the past without holding on to what causes harm. Our eating habits and body image reflect balance— no deprivation nor excess.

We enjoy time alone and appreciate time spent with those we love. We have a sense of "family" and a feeling of "belonging." We know the way home.

When we react solely on emotion, if we overindulge or become attached to stuff, if we judge on appearances only, the sacral chakra starts to chortle and chunk. Mild imbalances may contribute to resentments, feelings of guilt, or a sense of loneliness. Our cycles may become irregular, and we may feel "off." With increasing levels of disconnection, we forget who we are, lose our taste for life, and can feel burned out or numb. Psychically we may suffer insomnia, experience weight loss/gain, develop addiction, and have reproductive, hormone, and blood problems.

The color of the sacral chakra is orange.

As a standard, oranges, coppers, browns, and clears have a beneficial effect on the sacral charka.

SOLAR PLEXUS

Do you have power or does the world have power over you?

The third chakra formulates the impressions we have of ourselves and the imprint we leave on the world. From confidence to self-assurance to the belief that we can change and create our reality, the energy we exude pulses through the solar plexus chakra. Housing the liver, gall bladder, stomach, small intestines, and pancreas, this center allows us to process and contribute, with a personal touch, to the world. Sunny yellow and bright, the solar plexus is anchored just below the belly button and shines forward and back from the body.

When balanced, we feel a general sense of optimism and confidence. We can live in shades of color—refusing to judge the world as black or white. We set healthy boundaries, feel happy to say "yes" and at peace saying "no." We allow ourselves to learn and grow without demanding perfection or instantaneous results. We listen to others and accept differences. We know who we are and recognize our worth.

As we begin to entertain guilt and doubt, engage in self-reproach, overeat, or force ourselves to do things we really don't want to do, the solar plexus can spin off. We feel jaded, alone, victimized. If we continue to struggle, our digestion becomes sluggish, we may feel bloated, heavy, and bitter. Further imbalances can result in rage, ulcers, or a sense of helplessness.

The color of the solar plexus chakra is golden yellow.

Divinely, stones and specimens in gold, yellow, clear, copper, and bronze work steadily and quickly to restore order in our personal cosmos. As we work with this family, we discover imperfections truly enrich the journey of life.

HEART CHAKRA

Who do you love? Who loves you? Are you a lovey-dove?

The fourth chakra helps us adore life and share the good feels with those in our world. Our ability to express affection, feel lovable, and genuinely lift others comes from the fourth chakra. Good will, compassion, and generosity stem here. This center fuels the heart, lungs, lymph and immune systems, and well as the blood.

When balanced, we freely and genuinely express appreciation and love. This is not a "Hallmark" kind of sappy emotion (that's the job of the sacral charka), but rather, a deep and abiding sense of acceptance and gratitude for those about whom we care and a willingness to accept those on our path just as they are. We release control, graciously receive, and recognize Spirit in all life forms. We honor nature, appreciate diversity, and tend to little things. We demonstrate compassion and empathy.

As the heart chakra flags and falters, usually a result of self-judgement or feelings of separation, this energy center may express imbalance through cardiac issues, lung and breathing troubles, and autoimmune conditions. We begin to feel adversarial, lonely, and lost. In time, depression and apathy may ensue.

The colors of the heart chakra are green and pink.

Working with stones in the green, turquoise, pink, and clear families will bring ease and balance to the heart. Utilizing these crystals will gently, with measure, open our center and heal the wounds that can scar. When we connect with these stones, allowing ourselves to be nurtured, we awaken to the truth of our nature and embrace the gift of life.

THROAT CHAKRA

Speak or take the back seat?

Our fifth, or throat chakra, expertly handles, processes, and distributes communication in all its many expressions. From speech to gestures to music to what is unsaid, this center interprets language is all forms. Equally important, this chakra enables us to listen to others. What we hear not only comes from the outside, but messages are constantly communicated to us from within. How freely we express our individuality, whether through writing, speech, art, or personal style streams through this center.

The thyroid, neck, parathyroid glands, trachea, ears, jaws, teeth, mouth, nose and lower facial features all reside within the throat chakra.

When balanced, we let our truth express through all we do. From posture to conversations to listening to others and accepting their point of view, we stay in the moment and let messages flow. We discern what is ours to accept and reject what cannot serve. We feel clear, connected, able to speak up when it's time and stay quiet in turn. We embrace silence and are nonplussed by noise.

If we stifle our voice, experience oppression or abuse, or become conditioned as to what is "right" to say, our throat chakra begins to falter. We struggle with confidence, feel defeated in communication, and resign to shutting up. Conversely, we may overshare, command others, or attempt to bully or control. An imbalanced throat chakra may result in throat issues, thyroid disease, tooth and jaw troubles, sinus infections, or allergies.

The color of the throat chakra is light blue.

Gems and minerals with a tropical vibe help to ease a sore throat chakra. Blues, light greens, and clears open this chakra to freedom and balance. As we work with these treasures, we check our thoughts, trust our wisdom, and more readily speak from the heart.

THIRD EYE CHAKRA

Have you had your vision checked?

The sixth chakra provides a window to our world. Located over the forehead and including the eyes and eyebrows, this energy center allows us to see on the outside and dream within. It houses our memories, visions, hopes, and aspirations. Symbols and archetypes, collective understanding, and our ancestral heritage find home here. This center envelopes the pituitary gland, eyes, brain stem, and forehead.

When balanced, we willingly see the world each day through fresh eyes. We consider new possibilities and hold on to images that inspire growth. We dream, sometimes in color, sleep well, and find ourselves rested during the night. Seeing or holding a vision for others is a gift we can offer.

When unsettling images, violent pictures, and stagnant environments fill our eyes, we start to lose sight of who we are. As this happens, we struggle with insomnia, experience headaches, and no longer dream. Eye difficulty, head issues, and dizziness may occur. We feel challenged to find the light and fear darkness encroaching.

The color of the third eye chakra is indigo.

Thankfully, crystals and gems from the purple, indigo, deep blue, and gold families can help us re-open the window to the soul. These stones work powerfully and deeply to sweep away harmful images and restore our power to dream. With these minerals, our third eye chakra balances, clears, and finds peace within and with the world.

CROWN CHAKRA

Do you have a higher power?

The seventh and last of the major chakras resides atop the head and is our connection to all that is. The crown chakra processes and provides our spiritual outlook on the world. Encompassing the head, pineal gland, and upper brain, the soft spot of a baby is the open crown. This chakra is the point through which our soul enters and exits our body, the physical realm, when we emerge in birth and depart through death.

A balanced crown chakra allows us to reconcile the spiritual/emotional/physical journey of human life. We learn to grieve, feel compassion, and find hope. We can stay present while learning from the past and contemplating our future. Our understanding of spiritual practice as it relates to and differs from religion serves us in a positive manner. Tolerant of others and willing to embrace the mystery of life, we stand humble in an expansive Universe.

If we fall into extremes, attempt to find security through control, judge by differences, see separation over unity, the crown charka can weaken and clog. This imbalance may affect our head with achiness, dizziness, or pain. Hair loss will often occur as the imbalance becomes severe. Anger, loneliness, despair, and hopelessness may permeate as the crown chakra is further blocked.

The color of the crown chakra is purple.

In times of struggle, separation, or isolation, purples, clears, and tektites provide fresh air for the soul. These mineral families stabilize, clear, and energize the seventh chakra, helping us feel rejoined with the circle of life. With power and cohesion, crown opening crystals adorn us with the spirit of Life and the belief that we are designed to shine.

AURA HOUR

Your bubble. Personal space. The Field. An energy envelope.

The aura.

If we conceptualize the body and charkas like a house, the aura would be the yard. This energy sphere surrounds us in every direction from over the top of the head to several inches below the feet. If you were to stretch your arms fully, you would touch the outer edge of your auric field. Not static, the aura can expand and contract depending on what we eat or drink, how we think or feel, and where we live and work. Intricate, layered, and vibrant, the aura creates a space for our body and chakras to function.

The term energy "field" serves as a good description. When you move into a new house, the yard most likely had a few trees, some grass, maybe a bit of landscaping. This is like our aura when we incarnate. At the moment of birth, the aura comes complete with past life memories, habits and patterns, and our native tendencies. And, just like your yard, maintenance proves necessary. Cutting grass, pulling weeds, and bedding seeds keeps the outdoor living space neat. Clearing your aura with sage, salt baths, time outside, music, and prayers will keep your field fresh and tidy.

The thoughts we think, the beliefs we nurture, the habits we incorporate are like seeds we plant in the yard. This would be the truth of the statement, "You reap what you sow."

In addition, the aura hosts our angels, spirit guides, and ancestors. Our soul's blueprint, totem animals, and loved ones who have passed pop in on our energy bubble--sometimes you may feel like there's a party in your aura's yard! With so many rich spiritual essences percolating here, your aura works around the clock.

Perhaps you've been to a New Age shop or Psychic Fair and snapped a photo of your aura. The technology has come a long way over the past few years; my first energy picture was spit out by a polaroid looking camera. I had to wave it in the air to speed development.

The photograph may come with a report as to the color meanings and other spiritual info. These pictures tend to be reasonably accurate—at the moment they are taken. As you read the report, your aura will change. Go to the parking lot and receive a happy phone call—your aura will change. Stub your toe or get a speeding ticket---yep! Your aura will shift. Like reflections on rippling water, our energy reflects the constant nature of change.

To be sure, each of us tends to have a base color or a palate of colors permeating our aura consistently. Want to know yours? Think of your favorite color as a child or the color clothing in which you feel most confident. Most likely, this is the native color to your energy.

Here is an overview of the general meaning of aura colors:

White—indicates purity, innocence, and surrender into the Divine. Spiritual masters such as Mother Mary, Buddha, and Jesus are often depicted with brilliant, white auras.

Red—passion, intensity, strength, volume, vitality, zest, action. Red in the energy field often reflects "doing" over "being." When this passion has a spiritual inspiration, the red will shift to a neon pink hue. Cloudy red indicates depression, sadness, over-competitiveness, or anger.

Orange—sensuality, creativity, nurturance, domesticity. Orange hues in the aura typically occur in those who are deeply sensitive, shy, and highly artistic. A hearty appetite and robust desires manifest as orange tones. Muddy orange indicates over-indulgence, greed, secrecy, and sometimes guilt.

Yellow—optimism, confidence, happiness, wisdom, warmth. Yellow in the energy field indicates a natural exuberance and hopeful outlook on life. For those with a knack for spiritual advancement, yellow will frequently expand into a golden light. If struggling with insecurity, helplessness, poor diet or negative environments, yellow will cloud and appear a dark mustard brown.

Green—Earth angel, earth angel, will you be mine? This color in the aura indicates a nature lover and plant mom. Nurturing, calm, soothing, and healing, those who go green have a genuine love for the planet and for the inhabitants therein. From animals to people to plants to trees, appreciation for all life resonates with green. Dark, muddied green may indicate nature deprivation or a resistance to the physical world.

Light blue—easy breezy, pull up a chair and get cozy, chatting up a five-hour conversation (where did the time go?) is the essence of light blue. This color radiates from the throat center and lends an air of trustworthiness, charisma, and charm. Light blue opens a space for our hearts to feel safe going with the flow and learning as we go. Murky blue could indicate victimhood, suppression, confusion, or an identity crisis of some form.

Dark blue—dream a little dream. This color resonates with the air of sacred rites and ancient mysteries. Wisdom, power, inner vision, and profound presence radiate from indigo. Dull or heavy dark blue may indicate an excessive desire to control, severe depression, or insomnia.

Purple—hail your majesty. The shade of royalty and the crown chakra, this color indicates a deep connection to spirit and to the gift of life. Embracing a higher power, seeking deeper meaning, and yearning to understand what is beyond the ordinary pulsate from purple. Murky purple can indicate trauma relating to religion or a fractured connection to the concept of God.

Brown—infrequently seen in the aura under normal conditions, this usually indicates a depressed energy OR someone who is deeply connected to the fairy folk and elven kingdom.

Black—cloaked in darkness, black in the aura indicates a choice to suppress, hide, or escape. Black is not "bad" nor is it an "evil" color, however, it typically appears where imbalanced energy occurs.

The beauty of our aura lies in our relationship with it. Your energy field reflects you and affects you, but you can affect it, too.

For example, one Sunday afternoon I onlooked as my son splashed in a public pool. After a few minutes, I noticed a much larger person approach him in a seemingly confrontational manner. Watching nonverbal cues, I noted him shrinking back and displaying distress.

Not wanting to make matters worse, but knowing I had to do something, I decided to use my aura to shift the situation.

Taking a few deep breaths, I imagined filling my energy field like a balloon. Larger and larger it grew—think Good Year blimp circling over the Rose Bowl. I pictured intense colors shining brightly. I intended no harm, rather, a change in the dynamic and a peaceful conclusion between my son and the other person.

Within a few minutes, the person looked away, began chatting with someone and let my son be. I sent blessings to all and deflated the dirigible surrounding me.

On another occasion, I traveled in a faraway state with my kiddos. We stopped at a gas station to fill up the tank, and as I stepped out of the car I got smacked by funky vibes. Had resources been more plentiful, I would have pulled out of the station. Yet, out west, convenience stores dot the interstate like far flung stars in vast constellation. I needed fuel.

Not wanting to draw attention to myself, I opted to pull my aura in and cloak myself with an etheric blanket. With a few deep breaths, I imagined a dark purple and dark blue light enveloping my field. I kept my head up and eyes forward, and gently slipped into the store to pay.

No one, save the cashier, seemed to notice me. No one!

Upon returning to my car, I imagined taking the blanket off; I gave a little shake and shimmy to set things back in place. With a few easy breaths, I refilled my aura, just as I had my gas tank, with some unleaded color-fuel. This practice felt empowering and energizing.

Try it.

Humans don't have exclusive rights to the aura. Plants, planets, animals, abodes, forests, and fields—each is encapsulated in an energy field. Though the colors appear different, and the size varies significantly, every living being on our beautiful Earth emanates energy.

A basic working knowledge of the aura helps when utilizing the gift of crystals and stones. The vibrational energy of the mineral kingdom flows out from each specimen in every direction. Our body and chakras are benefitted as these waves flow inward, clearing and illuminating our field. Like little beacons, crystals transmit messages of hope, strength, and vitality in a timeless and timely fashion.

Choosing stones based on color is a wonderful way to honor our innate wisdom for self-healing. If you think you need purple, grab the amethyst, and trust it's the right stone. If you feel like green, let malachite enter the scene. Often, color deficiencies in our aura can be corrected with stones. Trust your gut.

Your aura is a beautiful space for your body and chakras. Let crystals bless you as you cherish the gift of you.

ROCKING AROUND THE CLOCK

The Weekday Grind

6am

PYRITE

Good morning, sunshine! This day is yours.

Pyrite is a sweet gem that infuses the aura with confidence, clarity, and cool-headed calm. Connected with the solar plexus chakra and the astrological sign of Leo, this stone, sometimes called "Fool's Gold" after its rich looking appearance, offers an energetic tether between you and your best self. Widely distributed and found on six continents, this sparkler ranges in price from pocket change to a fistful of large bills.

Pyrite will send your intentions forward into the light of day, providing a sense of presence that enhances recognition of coincidences, synchronicities, and signs. Additionally, it turns up the volume of your inner voice—because sometimes we tune out our whispering wisdom when the world loudly shouts. Pyrite assists in easily hearing intuition so we act as your own advocate and choose our best interests.

This gem instills a sense of grace, diplomacy, and nobility, inspiring you to treat all around you with dignity and respect. With pyrite, Love rules.

Pyrite will set your energy in motion with confidence, creativity, courage, and motivation to manifest desires. Not only that, but it bolsters optimism and positivity to push us along the path with a Midas touch. Focus, determination, will, and power unite as we get our soul's work done well.

This nugget heralds a bright new dawn where you will shine. Rise up and stand strong.

Affirmation:

I will create a day I love.

7am

YELLOW CALCITE

Just like the soft glow of the morning sun, yellow (or honey) calcite gently emanates a wonderful vibe that uplifts the entire energy field. Calcites are so named because of their large calcium content. This mineral occurs in a rainbow of colors, depending on inclusions, and is widely distributed throughout our world. Because it is common, stocking up on calcite will bless without breaking the bank.

All calcites, and especially yellow, emanate, a friendly, cheery vibe. Imagine the person or pet in your life who always makes you smile, who knows just the right words, who cools you when you're hot and warms you when you feel out in the cold. Calcite is the crystalline expression of that special someone.

This feel-good vibe occurs because calcites work to open and align the first, third, and sixth chakras. These energy centers keep us centered, confident, and clear. Dipped into that honey goodness with calcite, we allow our best selves to rise.

With its yellow hue, honey calcite works specifically and deeply on the third charka, also called the solar plexus. This is the seat of our self-esteem, our mental processes, and our sense of personal power in the world. As it moves through the solar plexus, a sense of assuredness, presence, clarity, balance, and centeredness will come. Additionally yellow calcite sparks creativity and clears out old, limiting beliefs. The pain and anger of the past hold you back no more!

This stone can complement the liver's natural process of detoxifying the body. It may help the small intestines with absorption of the best nutrients. Because it bears calcium, it strengthens hair, teeth, nails, and bone.

Not bad for a little rock.

Affirmation:

My body and mind are balanced, nurtured, and clear.

8am

CLEAR QUARTZ

Three cheers for clear quartz!

If I were stranded on a desert island and could only tote one stone, my choice would be clear—clear quartz. Widely distributed, easy to find, available at every price and size, clear quartz does it all.

Expect laundry.

Like a diamond, clear quartz attracts and reflects light in all facets of life. First, its essence moves into our energy field through the crown chakra, connecting to the Spirit of we are and the frequency of life. From here, perspectives on God, divine presence, and our soul's work come into clear view.

From the moment of birth, we are connected to Source. Children easily and readily believe in "magic" because they've not been conditioned to limit beliefs or fix themselves to rigid thoughts. That beautiful innocence and sheer purity of mind aligns with the essence of quartz and the crown chakra. When we accept Spirit, we become open to a life of miracles, magic, and Love beyond words.

Quartz brings soft, pulsing waves of peace that course from the head and down the entire body. As this happens, the vibration of clear quartz sloughs off any dusty, old energy and protects with radiant light. This gem heightens awareness, enhances memory, boosts energy, and elicits a sense of well-being.

On a physical level, clear quartz reinforces our organ systems that run healthily and catalyzes those that flag to grow stronger. This whole-body approach can be especially helpful when are run down or always on the go.

Clear quartz may enhance intuition and help call to mind relationships, modalities, and experiences that can support us on the path. This stone is a perfect friend to carry when you're feeling run down.

And if all this isn't enough, clear quartz also senses and releases any unconscious blocks that may hold us back. So long self-sabotage, goodbye self-doubt—there's a new, wonderful energy that abounds.

Affirmation:

The goodness of my soul radiates from me and into the world.

9am

GARNET

Confession time: My initial reason for working with garnet came from vanity; this lovely gem has been touted for centuries for its anti-aging properties and the playful spirit it sparks. Behold the Fountain of Youth in crystal form.

Good looks aside, garnet is essential for your collection as it will serves well in many wonderful ways. Relatively common and mined in Asia, Africa, North America, and South America, garnet can be found in price ranges from very affordable to top dollar.

Deep red to black in color, garnet fortifies the will, centers the mind, and energizes the body. Working with this stone brings a feeling of protection, like carrying a little shield. Garnet also enhances circulation and the flow of energy throughout the body, infusing confidence, courage, and optimism. The fortifying effects of garnet may bolster the circulatory system—improving blood flow, stabilizing vessel walls, and strengthening the heart.

Physically, garnet can strengthen muscle recovery after workouts, help with kidney issues, regulate cycles, and ease menstrual cramps.

Thanks to its resonance with the root, solar plexus, heart, and crown chakras, garnet can move us into the beautiful alignment of mind, body, and soul. A delightful surge of divine life force emanates from this gemstone.

Garnet has rich and wonderful traditions in our history; this stone was used by the High Priests in Israel and by the Pharaohs in Egypt. Carrying garnet will tap into these powerful and sacred legacies. Toss into your collection this tried-and-true tool and harness ancient energies for the modern world.

Affirmation:

I am protected and empowered by the might of angels.

10am

GREEN AVENTURINE

Fabulous and flecked with crystalline sparkles, green aventurine is not only a stunning stone, but also considered a lucky charm. With its soft color and glorious sheen, this lovely has a relaxing and calming effect on the entire energy field. Aventurine comes in a variety of colors and is widely distributed through Asia and South America, making this lovely treasure accessible and affordable.

Working with aventurine allows for the slow and steady opening of the heart. With a Goldilocks pace, green aventurine helps you receive in just the right portions while simultaneously expanding your sense of worthiness. As this happens, you become more naturally receptive to and trusting of good that comes.

With a balanced heart chakra, we notice synchronicities, coincidences, and intuitive nudges happening with increased frequency. This is the "magic" of green aventurine—when we are aligned with our heart, readily receiving what we love, we feel good! The Universe's natural state is that of abundance, creativity, and endless expansion. Our job is simply to appreciate, align, and receive from this incredible font of good.

Additionally, with a wonderfully open heart, we easily experience compassion, empathy, and patience with ourselves and others. In this natural state of grace and feeling of bliss, we are positioned as leaders, an inspiration to others. We feel qualified to make decisions in our own best interest.

Physically, this jewel may assist the body's immune and lymphatic systems, soothe asthma and other breathing conditions, and enhance the effectiveness of our circulatory system.

Green aventurine brings out the best in us and calls us to honor the innate divinity in all of life.

Affirmation:

I am primed and poised to receive my good.

11am

BLUE TOURMALINE

Tourmaline is a hard-working mineral that comes in a wide assortment of colors. No matter the hue, one of the therapeutic benefits of tourmaline is soothing and grounding our energy and clearing away all the extraneous noise, thoughts, and judgments. Located in Asia, Africa, North and South America, tourmaline appears in a variety of colors and price ranges. With so many beautiful and accessible options, you're sure to find the right stone for wallet and soul.

As I kid, I had a toy, similar to an Etch-a-Sketch, called Mr. Wiggles. This poor guy had no hair at all—a big cue ball. Using a magnet stylus and magnetic shavings, Mr. Wiggles could take on different looks: a mustache here, a mohawk there, some crazy eyebrows to set him apart. Then, with a tilt of the board, he was bald again. Until next time…

Imagine that all the noise and chaos, the images and impressions you're exposed to throughout the day as magnetic shavings piling up and weighing you down. Tourmaline "tilts the board" and sloughs the particles off your field. Cleared from you, this energy returns to the earth where it is replenished and recycled into something new. And I promise, tourmaline will never give you a beard or crazy hair do!

Another benefit, tourmaline helps us discover inner truths and unconscious beliefs. When we feel assured of who we are, we feel more ease in expressing our wants and needs. If you struggle with self-expression or feel lost about how to implement self-care, tourmaline can serve you well.

Physically, this mineral may heal the thyroid, boost metabolism, and resynchronize our body's internal communication system. Issues like insomnia and anxiety, shortness of breath or helplessness can be relieved using blue tourmaline.

Affirmation:

I dust off the past and unshackle my fears. I am free.

Noon

CITRINE

Citrine is powerful and pretty. Sunny bright and honey warm, this stone helps banish the blahs, cheer you when your confidence flags, sweep away toxins, and obliterate mental blocks. I like using citrine around the lunch hour as it keeps the "hangry" feelings in check and helps rev up metabolism.

Found in Asia, Africa, Europe, North and South America, this mineralogic beauty comes at a decent price. When shopping for citrine, be aware that some distributors will sell heat-treated amethyst as citrine. When choosing an authentic piece, look for a pale-yellow color. Stones bright orange or intense yellow are not naturally occurring citrine. Knowledge is power; now you know how to spot the fake and grab the citrine gold.

Citrine helps bolster the first three chakras. These energy centers keep us grounded, centered, and aligned with the individual work we accomplish in our lives. As such, citrine inspires feelings of calm, confidence, and a willingness to trust our emotions as we go with the flow.

This stone also helps us tune in to our "gut feelings" with more acuity; when the junk is discarded, we more readily hear the wisdom in our body and soul. Citrine facilitates a deeper connection to our personal will, our unique mission, and how we can speak up for what we need and want.

One of the qualities I most love about citrine is that it helps define creative impulses. For example, if you feel hungry, but don't have a craving, citrine will shine the light on what your body most needs. If you want to learn an instrument, but don't know which is best, this crystal will allow you to "know" the right one.

Another therapeutic benefit of citrine is its knack for pushing us out of our own way. If you want something but deprive yourself, if you need something but deny yourself, this crystal will short circuit your ego, so you have love in your life in every form.

Physically, citrine may promote healthy digestion, ease bloating, help the body regulate blood sugar, and reduce junk food cravings. It can also assist in clearing some skin conditions.

Citrine amplifies our ability to manifest and our readiness to receive. Consistently loving and truly powerful, this crystal will get the job done.

Affirmation:

I have a clear head and a confident heart.

1pm

DOLOMITE

Oh my goodness, I will never forget the first time I saw dolomite. Peaches and cream and bumpy-rough, this nurturing creature is ooey-gooey goodness disguised as a rock.

One summer afternoon, while browsing a local crystal shop, I spotted a special someone out of the corner of my eye. I grabbed it up, not recognizing it by sight, but knowing I just had to lay hands on this lovey. I felt a warm and soft sensation pass through me. For a moment, I got a bit spacey; I wanted to let that feeling stay a while. Too quickly, I awkwardly realized other customers were looking at me. With a goofy smile, I floated up to the checkout stand to buy my new rock.

With my work as a medium, I move between two worlds. Half of my consciousness resides in the spirit world, chatting it up with Loved Ones on the Other Side. The other half is sitting on the Earth relaying messages from beyond. At times, I experience a bit of strain coming back into the "ordinary" world and my digestion gets sluggish, my vision will blur, and I feel a bit out of sorts.

Dolomite relieved this for me. When I hold this stone, my spirit lines back up with my body, and I feel "set" to go.

Dolomite balances all the chakras. It softens the edges, smooths the rough spots, melts the blocks.

Gently, it steadies us in place and eases us into the flow. Using this stone after lunch, when we have to get back to work, switch gears, or overcome the early afternoon lull assists us in feeling at peace wherever we are.

Physically, dolomite works with the digestive system, pancreas, liver, gall bladder, and esophagus. It may be helpful in relieving ulcers, skin disruptions, and mouth issues.

This stone is perfect for children and pets. Simply place it in a bedroom, especially in situations where anxiety persists, or fear lingers. Dolomite promotes calm, emanating into the environment waves of stillness. With dolomite, peace will prevail for all.

Affirmation:

I take a moment to relax and settle in. My body and spirit are aligned for good.

2pm
TIGER'S EYE

One glance at this stone and you'll be mesmerized. Banded layers of orange, golden, dark brown, and copper create captivating patterns that invoke the spirit of its namesake. Mined in South Africa, India, the US, and Australia, this beauty is easy to find at a price to pounce on.

Tiger's Eye is appropriately named not just because of its appearance, but also based on how it works in our energy field. This stone protects, strengthens, and energizes. It assists with balance—both physical and emotional, and boosts discernment, decisiveness, and our ability to make good use of resources.

In a world offering an overwhelming myriad of options, we can become unclear, ambivalent, overloaded and shut down. Tiger's eye spurs clarity, action, and quick adaptability. Our spiritual agility guides us as we roar, purr, and prowl through the jungle of the afternoon.

This stone sparks our senses in such a way that we learn to savor the experience of life. From glorious sunsets to sumptuous foods to melodious music, tiger's eye hones our awareness in on that which is good.

Physically, tiger's eye helps regulate cycles, may ease constipation, and helps with fluid balance. It can also support improved circulation to the lower extremities and could reduce phantom pain and neuropathy.

Tiger's eye assists mediation and diplomatic communication in work and home life. It grounds us into our mission and helps us feel centered in who we are. With acuity and clarity, we choose wisely under the careful watch of tiger's eye.

Affirmation:

I listen to my intuition and act in ways that are inspired, fair, and wise.

3pm

POPPY JASPER

Jasper is a group of stones that come in a variety of colors and various shapes and forms. The hue of each is determined by the mineral's inclusions.

Jaspers includes such treasures as Rainforest, red, picture, dalmatian, zebra, giraffe, mook, and more. Plentifully distributed worldwide, jasper is easy to find and reasonably priced.

For the most part, jaspers work with the lower charkas in tortoise-like fashion---slow and steady wins the race. When placed in a room, jasper gently and consistently holds and maintains a positive vibe, like an energetic welcome mat, warmly greeting all who enter. When worn, jasper releases subtle waves of peace; not too little but not too much.

Poppy jasper rocks the boat.

As the name implies this mineral kicks energy into high gear. Caffeine without the buzz, poppy jasper will give you a boost when you need it most.

Poppy's effect starts in the root chakra, where it centers and stabilizes our connection to Mother Earth. With a powerful whoosh, this stone opens the flow of energy between us and nature. Enhancing vitality, strength, and centeredness, this gem sends waves of energy to our second chakra. Here, we feel a delightful and uplifting surge of good chi and high vibes. All is well.

On a physical level, poppy jasper helps strengthen digestion, promote elimination, revitalize the kidneys, and boost circulation to the lower extremities. When faced with chaos, this jewel brings cohesion and focus.

The crystal kick is effective for 20-30 minutes and can be experienced each time poppy jasper is held. Forgo the coffee and Red Bull, let this stone lift you.

Affirmation:

A delightful surge of divine energy fills me now.

4pm

AMAZONITE

As the afternoon begins to wind down, having a stone to keep our spirit high and our thoughts focused seems ideal, and amazonite fits the bill. With a seafoam green hue, this wonderful gem soothes the heart and throat, calms the nervous system, and releases negative energy that we've picked up through the day. This gentle gem brews a perfect blend as we transition from afternoon to evening. Found in China, South Africa, Russia, India, and the US, it is slightly less common but well worth the investment.

Considered in many ancient cultures a "lucky stone" or the "gambler's stone," amazonite aligns all of us--chakras, heart and mind, emotions, and thoughts with Universal Love. In this state, balanced and clear, we naturally flow with the abundance of life. Rather than relying on happenstance or chance, amazonite aligns us synchronistically in the glorious flow of good. Who needs luck when you've got Spirit in you, moving through you, providing every need to you?

Amazonite allows us to share our thoughts and feelings with assuredness and a sense of calm. Often communication breaks down when emotions drown words. Amazonite leverages this, letting the emotions surface in a way that supports communication. This stone helps us speak our truth without hesitation or reservation with a sense of calm. Carrying amazonite is a powerful way to activate these traits.

Placing a small piece at your workspace can speed manifestation of good.

On a physical level, this stone may improve circulation, help with liver function, support adequate hydration, and healthy respiration. Amazonite may also enhance the lymphatic systems ability to keep us healthy and on the go.

Amazonite brings change---change for good.

Affirmation:

I express and manifest my heart's desires in all aspects of my life.

5pm

SMOKY QUARTZ

If I had a magic wand, it would be comprised of smoky quartz.

This stone is a true beauty. Part of the quartz family, the "smoke" in this mineral is a result of natural irradiation. From gray to brown to black, each piece of smoky quartz is unique and wonderful.

Widely distributed across our planet, smoky quartz can be readily obtained at a reasonable price. With the strength of a mountain and the might of the sun, smoky works consistently, powerfully, and unfailingly to help.

This mineral friend recognizes and releases any energy from our aura that is unsupportive in any way; you don't need to know how the junk got there or where it will go. Smoky quartz is the ultimate cleaning service— transforming the old into the fabulous truth of YOU. Willingly release and readily believe; one call does it all.

After clearing all the junk, smoky quartz anchors our energy to the heart of the Earth, infusing us with might and trust. Additionally, each chakra is cleared and opened so we feel ready to face the world with poise, centeredness, and a spirit of calm.

On the physical body, smoky quartz acts as a mild analgesic. If struggling with minor aches or pains, tensions or strains, smoky quartz will promote cellular oxygenation and clean up. This mineral may also assist with absorption of micronutrients, vitamins, and minerals.

A perfect piece to use after work and before beginning evening or family time, smoky quartz smooths transitions and keeps us well.

Affirmation:

I accept the best and release the rest. I am strong.

6PM

GREEN JADE

Known in the East as "The Supreme Nurturer," green jade has been revered as a sacred and prized stone for centuries. Distributed widely and occurring in purple, white, red, black, and blue, jade proves readily obtainable and reasonably priced. With a lovely pale to deep green hue, jade blesses and benefits the heart. Gentle and good, this prize is suitable for children and pets, too.

Green jade helps us fall in love with life. To be clear, an abiding reverence for life doesn't imply reveling in challenging circumstances, nor projecting a pretense of a picture perfect, hunky-dory life. Instead, jade helps us connect with an inner goodness, an innate innocence that buoys us in storms. By calling forth a vision of the fullness and richness of the Earth, we discover a Garden of Eden in our corner. From flowers to trees, our planet teems with beauty and abundance. Jade settles us so we feel blessed.

Jade, like a fertilizer, catalyzes growth and fosters good health. Believed to yield healing properties for the skin, muscles, eyes, blood vessels, ligaments, and tendons, jade straightens out all the rough, wrinkled spots. When emotions freeze or dreams stagnate, this stone gradually infuses renewal and regeneration.

Jade may ease reactive airway conditions and relieve the symptoms of carpal tunnel syndrome and TMJ. Our bodies are designed to thrive in the world. Jade reminds us that we are whole.

Be nurtured and loved into the evening with a profound knowing that all is well.

Affirmation:

My heart is strong and my will is clear. I radiate vitality.

7pm

HOWLITE

Named after the geologist who first identified it, howlite is mined across the globe, occurs in a variety of colors, and is easily acquired at a reasonable cost.

Think of howlite as a multivitamin for your aura. Because it resonates with the crown chakra, this mineral works on your whole being—body, mind, and soul. First, howlite bathes us in a feeling of quiet contentment and washes us in a sense of calm. As this happens, we settle into our bodies and the heart rate slows, breathing deepens, and muscles relax. With a centered and calm body, howlite next works to open our mind, facilitating learning, assisting with memory, and enhancing study skills. Howlite not only aids in retaining facts but incorporating knowledge into a usable form.

This mineral fosters motivation and confidence and lends a sense of encouragement as we take steps toward our goals.

Physically, howlite strengthens bones, teeth, and connective tissues. It may promote oxygenation and enhance circulation to soft tissues. Placing howlite on scar tissue may help reduce redness and "pulling" on the area.

Beyond personal benefits, howlite blesses our environment, too. Placing a piece clears a room of negative energies; this stone is ideally housed where the family relaxes or in common areas. Since it promotes peace, howlite works well in a bedroom, even tucked under a pillow, particularly in times of insomnia or when bad dreams prevail.

Howlite beautifully ushers in the twilight energy and primes for a satisfying evening. Savor this stone as you connect.

Affirmation:

A pleasant, peaceful environment welcomes, inspires, and supports me.

8pm

BLOODSTONE

Bloodstone is part of the chalcedony family and is sometimes called Heliotrope. This stone is distributed worldwide and is reasonably priced. Bloodstone proves a wonderful ally in times of reflection, contemplation, and when focus is required.

Easy to recognize, bloodstone is so named because of its red spots. Since ancient times, bloodstone has served as a potent talisman—warding away negativity and invoking the power of our divinity. With a majestic air, bloodstone invites and welcomes us home to our body. When we are set and settled, we feel comfortable relaxing, reflecting, and releasing events of the day with a peaceful heart and calm mind.

After entreating us into our body, bloodstone begins to purify and realign our cells, declutter thoughts and ease our spirit. As this happens, we experience encouragement and strength on all levels.

Physically, this mineral may ease conditions such as anemia, low blood counts, irregular or heavy menstrual bleeding, and swollen gums. It may improve blood flow to the kidneys and mitigate the effects of poor circulation from conditions such as diabetes. Placing a small piece on cold hands or feet may encourage a warming sensation. Bloodstone may stimulate appetite and metabolism after stress or surgery.

Like howlite, bloodstone's energy radiates into the environment, clearing and uplifting any old or stagnant energies around us.

With grace, bloodstone centers us in our highest selves, moving us into a place where we can rest, restore, and dream.

Affirmation:

My body is strong, steady, and stable. I feel good.

9pm

MOONSTONE

Oh moonstone! This glorious being comes in many colors and has been used for adornment as far back as Roman times. Rightly named, this quiet beauty reflects light and seems to glow. Looking at moonstone and its many faces relaxes the mind and summons the imagination. Tranquil and serene, moonstone embodies femininity.

Moonstone naturally occurs in a variety of colors thanks to a miscellany of inclusions from different parts of the world. Black, rainbow, cat's eye, blue, and white are a few hues. The price point varies widely from color to color; for this reason, I encourage you to choose the kind of moonstone that resonates with you.

After experiencing the physical blessings of bloodstone in the eight o'clock hour, moonstone flawlessly prepares us for sleep and rest time.

Relaxing soft tissues, clearing cellular debris, enhancing blood flow to the endocrine glands, and balancing the kidneys, moonstone may illicit a relaxation effect in the entire body.

Once freed from the fast-paced pressures of the day, moonstone's effect may be felt on the spiritual level--enhancing intuition, calling forth wisdom and vision, and stirring our wonder for the mystery of life. This gem allows us to fall in rhythm with our inner cycles, discovering the truth of who we are.

Tasting the flavorful richness of our emotions allows us to feel peace with the ebb and flow of life. Rather than judging emotions as good or bad, right or wrong, moonstone lifts us to a place where we can learn from them all. This sets the stage for restful sleep and vivid dreams.

Moonstone offers the perfect tonic as we prepare for bed.

Affirmation:

My emotions are balanced and my intuition clear. I relax into the flow.

10pm

AMETHYST

Pouring out deep purple juiciness, amethyst opens our awareness to the endless, eternal beings that we are. With pulses of violet light of the highest spiritual frequency, this stone surrounds and fills us with sublime, divine energy.

Often referred to as "The Soul Stone," amethyst is part of the quartz family. Ancient Egyptians, Greeks, and Europeans used and revered this beautiful gem. Rightfully so, as amethyst protects during times of transition and illuminates the path that serves us best. Unearthed in North and South America, Russia, and parts of Africa, amethyst is affordable and obtainable at most crystal shops.

One of the most prized gifts of amethyst is its ability to soothe and calm the nervous system. As we anchor into the Truth of life, we begin to access a powerful place of stillness that transcends the ordinary world. From this place, we grow our intuition, release addictions, tap into motivation, and come to an acceptance of the trials and triumphs of life. This dazzler will always bless you, lift you, and allow you to see more fully who you are.

On the physical level, amethyst may ease headaches, tooth pain, TMJ, and can help lower blood pressure. It can boost the immune system in times of stress. Amethyst may also improve recovery after surgery or when rebounding from chronic illness.

This gem may help those with ALS, MS, aneurysms, dementia, or history of stroke.

Placing amethyst under your pillow will promote restful and rejuvenating sleep. It helps dream recall and may catalyze astral travel. When worn near the heart, this stone grants us the ability to access focus and decision-making abilities. With these qualities, our sense of personal power and global connection grow by leaps and bounds.

Amethyst is a genuine treasure in our world.

Affirmation:

I trust the flow of life. I am always connected to Love.

11pm

ROSE QUARTZ

After the purification and fortification provided by amethyst, rose quartz wraps you up tucks you in with sweet hugs of Divine Love.

This lovely stone, part of the quartz family, gleans its pink hue from inclusions of titanium, iron, and manganese. This stone is found on every continent except Antarctica and can be picked up for pocket change at any rock shop.

From shades deep to pale, rose quartz works on all levels of the heart. Timeless in its reach, it lifts old wounds and seeds future hopes as it prepares the heart, with each breath, to receive the ever-present gift of love.

The powerfully gentle vibration radiating from rose quartz is not the fleeting whim of romantic poets. Instead, this stone, bearing the strength of its metal-based inclusions, nourishes us with unconditional love. This experience is beyond mere pleasantry; divine love transcends personal attachments and relationships of the world. From family to friends to coworkers to neighbors to self, this force lifts us out of the ordinary and places us in the Heart of Source. Here, we don't have to hold on to guilt, resentment, or pain; we simply let Love be.

And love is always enough.

Within our bodies, rose quartz may promote the relaxation response by helping prompt decreased heart rate and a deeper breathing pattern. This may be of benefit for those struggling with asthma, anxiety, or COPD. Rose quartz may offer a soothing effect on the muscular system and promote kidney perfusion.

Dropping into the rose quartz essence of Divine love offers peace, calm, and assuredness. This is the perfect pillow to rest our heads at night

Affirmation:

I feel the gentle essence of love surrounding me now.

Midnight
SELENITE

Sometimes referred to as "The Stone of Light," selenite is a member of the gypsum family. This stone is unique for many reasons beyond its physical structure. Procured from Australia, Europe, Mexico, and the US, this mineral is readily obtainable at a low cost.

Selenite is a self-cleansing stone. Where other minerals and crystals benefit from clearing and charging, selenite keeps tidy and fresh all on its own. What's more, selenite can be used to clear all other crystals and rebalance their energies. This places selenite in a league of its own.

Selenite owes its name to the goddess of the moon, Selene. Gazing upon it, you will understand why. Much like our night companion, selenite possesses a radiant, glowy nature that enchants the eyes and expands the mind.

Because of this connection, selenite is considered a stone of the goddess: mysterious, creative, and wise. Selenite allows us to access the unseen and vibrant inner world as well as the outer bounds of our soul. With selenite's assistance, our dreams are revealed, and our wisdom becomes powerful, clear insight.

As we sleep, selenite promotes deep rest and tranquility within our body, while our soul can travel and access spiritual information far and wide. Under the guise of this crystal, we have a greater ability to recall and discern our dream time experiences and apply them in our waking world.

Physically, selenite may foster mineral absorption and utilization by the muscles and bones. It could be helpful to ease water retention and to regulate menstrual cycles. Additionally, this gem may ease challenges during childbirth and post-partum. Selenite may also ease the body's stress response during times of prolonged tension.

Selenite blesses with a peaceful night's rest—a moonbeam cloaked in a stone.

Affirmation:

As I rest, my body, mind, and spirit harmonize with heaven and earth. All is well.

1am

BLUE LACE AGATE

Simply gazing upon blue lace agate ushers feelings of peace and tranquility. Soft blue with delicate waves of white, this strong and able member of the agate family provides an effectual lift in our communicative abilities. Harvested in South Africa and Europe, this lovely is reasonably priced and obtainable from most rock shops.

Blue lace agate opens the throat chakra with gentle rays of empowering energy. In this space, affirmations become our truth, our intentions become our principles, and our ability to access angelic and divine guidance amplifies. This stone fosters the power to make intuition clear.

Using this gem at night is particularly beneficial when the noise and distractions of an ordinary day fade away. Without all the mind chatter and inner resistance, blue lace agate readily and steadily heals, balances, and fortifies confidence in how we've used our words. Whether giving public talks, singing for a crowd, or negotiating family chores, having an assured and easy style of communication grows our willingness to trust the flow of life. As we overcome the need to prove, justify, or defend our thoughts, beliefs, and decisions, we open to new ideas and forms of support.

Further, this stone provides a sense of acceptance and peace with the circumstances, situations, and conversations of the day. Rather than reliving what could have, should have, or might have been, blue lace agate fosters a spirit of reconciliation with what was so that we can relax and let go.

By boosting our connection with the spiritual realms, we remember messages from our dreams and understand how these messages apply in our lives. Blue lace agate is the key that unlocks the language of symbolism.

Physically, this gem eases inflammation, whether in joints or in tissues. This can be helpful for any arthritic or musculoskeletal conditions. It may enhance thyroid, lymph, and immune functions.

Promoting peace and gifting us with grace, blue lace agate is a nurturing and competent stone.

Affirmation:

I am serene and safe. I can let go.

2am

AZURITE

Like the depths of the oceans blue, azurite, sometimes called "The Stone of Heaven," casts our energy into the dreamy heart of our soul. Running deep like still waters, this rich, true-blue gem can immerse us into fathomless feelings of peace, tranquility, and relief. Mined in Australia, China, Chile, Russia, and the US, this beauty prices moderately and populates most specialty rock shops.

Because the color of azurite nearly matches our sixth, or 3rd eye chakra, and blends with the violet light of the crown chakra, azurite reminds us that we are part of the infinite cosmos. This feeling enhances our vision, expands our wisdom, and grows brilliant insight into who we are.

Swiftly, this stone releases images, impressions, or traumatic experiences that plague us. Azurite will help us "unsee" fear that holds us back as we illuminate the truth of who we are. This benefits us as we navigate dark and dreary circumstances in our daily lives. The world can be gloomy, yet azurite shines the light of hope.

Our eyes often blind us to the true beauty and mystery of life. Azurite awakens spiritual vision so we can more readily see all that is good.

On the physical level, this stone may relieve headaches, stress, and enhance dream recall. It may clear sinus and eye issues, can enhance neurotransmitter production and uptake, and ease TJM. Azurite may unbind tight muscles in the head and neck with peaceful pulsations of spiritual energy.

This gem proves a beautiful companion to use during meditation or contemplation.

Psychic development often rapidly accelerates with azurite as its powerful and coherent resonance lifts us from the ordinary into the unabashed miracle of who we are.

Affirmation:

My vision is clear, and my dreams are meaningful.

3am

LAPIS LAZULI

After delving into the depths with azurite, lapis lazuli handily and sturdily anchors us into the heart of the Universe and lifts us into assured spiritual self-confidence. Where azurite reveals wisdom, lapis inspires awareness of and inspiration for action steps to take in the waking world. Extracted from the Middle East, Russia, and South America, this gem's cost is low and obtainability is high.

The energy of lapis resonates with the first, fresh light of dawn. While primarily true blue, lapis is uniquely prized for its characteristic gold flecks and sparkles. This reminds us that we are here to be light in the world.

Lapis unveils strides we can make and a pace we can take that will amplify our ability to manifest and recognize our good. In areas where energy is blocked, this stone reveals the true cause and spiritual cure. With this, the vibration of lapis allows us to compassionately observe disharmony or dis-ease within ourselves or our relationships without feeling the urge to judge, doubt, resent, or regret. No need to cling to these emotions as they can only dampen our hearts. Compassion, enriched by lapis, frees us to be who we are.

Another gift of lapis lazuli is its power to activate our deeper sense of and trust in diving timing. In our instant gratification, drive-thru world, we often stifle growth with impatience. This stone allows us to rest assured, to trust that all things, everything, happens at the divine right time.

Within our physical body, lapis may ease migraines and sinus headaches. Neurologic conditions such as dementia, MS, insomnia, and hormone disorders may be relieved with this stone. Lapis may also help balance our appetite and promote healthy digestion and elimination and well as resync us with our innate rhythms and cycles.

Our time on earth is a dance of work and rest, give and receive, dream and do. Lapis takes to the dance floor and partners with us as we waltz through life.

Affirmation:

Divine wisdom is activated within me. I see with new eyes.

4am

RHODONITE

Rhodonite's name comes from the Greek words meaning "rose red." This lovely and gentle stone's moniker neatly conveys the energy it betroths. A stone of love, rhodonite opens our heart and root chakras and allows us to feel safe, connected, and lovable.

This gem is distributed worldwide, making it easy to obtain at a reasonable price. Usually pink with black streaks, rhodonite can reveal our hidden talents and grow the confidence to share these gifts with the world. When we feel anchored and secure, our willingness to open, our readiness to trust, and our ability to gift others amplifies. Rhodonite brings these feelings to heart and mind.

Using this stone as the night gives way to the dawn opens a space for us to begin integrating gently into the waking world. As we sleep, our soul may wander, explore, and journey to the edges of the cosmos. When it's time to get up, our energy must be properly "fitted" to home—the physical body. As rhodonite opens the root and heart chakra, our soul is furnished with a welcome mat and an open door. This facilitates a peaceful morning, ready recall of dreams, and a general sense of optimism for the new day.

On the physical level, rhodonite facilitates the production and recycling of blood cells, perhaps offsetting conditions such as anemia. It may ease menstrual cramps and foster healing of skin conditions.

When a wound is sustained, rhodonite may speed the healing process and mute the tendency to scar. This stone is also beneficial in normalizing blood pressure and cardiac function. It can also aid in the prevention of blood clots and may mitigate the possibility of spider or varicose veins.

Rhodonite buffers and blocks chaos and negativity so that we stay open to the truth and watchful for the good in life and the world. Its essence lifts the heart and fosters our growth.

Affirmation:

I open my heart and I accept my body as an expression of Spirit. I am whole.

5am

CARNELIAN

Carnelian is Vitamin C for the soul. Ranging in color from deep orange to a vibrant red, this stone is a member of the chalcedony family. Often called the "Stone of Optimism," this sweet rock will allow you to happily embrace a new day as the brilliant sun begins to rise. Widely distributed, this gem can be found in any rock shop at a decent price.

With its energy tuning and opening the first, second, and third chakras, carnelian helps us feel at home in our body, centered with our feet on the ground. As this occurs, we feel vital and strong, courageous, and stable. Building on this energy, carnelian opens us to creative ventures, abundant manifestations, and wild appreciation for all we have and are. Next, carnelian stimulates focus, confidence, memory retention, and our readiness to act. All this before getting out of bed!

On the physical level, this stone has the wonderful ability to detoxify and cleanse the body. Whether from poor eating habits, environmental pollution, or chronic stress, carnelian supports our body in breaking down and eliminating harmful substances of any kind. Not only that, but it amplifies our appetite for the foods, relationships, and situations that are for our best good.

Further, carnelian may balance reproductive issues, promote fertility, enhance muscle recovery after working out, and help build new neuromuscular bridges. This is helpful when learning a new skill such as knitting, yoga, playing an instrument, or dancing. Carnelian is a study buddy stone.

Carnelian can be used anytime a bad habit or old craving begins to detract or deter us. Its pure goodness will remind us that we deserve health, wellbeing, and a playful, happy journey through life.

Carnelian is sunshine for the soul.

Affirmation:

I joyfully accept my body as a sacred place on Mother Earth. I am here for good.

ROCKING AROUND THE CLOCK

Weekend Warriors

6am

SHUNGITE

Glossy black, shungite is a mineral comprised primarily of graphite, widely distributed, and found in a variety of shapes and sizes. From pyramids to wands to spheres, shungite's structure lends well to creative sculpting. Mined from Russia, this treasure is affordable and easily obtained at rock shops.

Working on the entire energy body, starting with our connection to Earth and moving up through the crown chakra, shungite positively affects all we are. As it vibrates, shungite weaves a net of protection from harmful EMFs, wicks out toxins, and then re-stabilizes the aura. This sets the stage for a smooth transition from sleep to wake as we are welcomed to a clear and centered body, mind, and soul.

Healing properties of shungite are especially helpful after a restless night, when experiencing bad dreams, or in times when physical discomfort has disrupted sleep as it shakes off the dark and welcomes the light.

This stone can provide additional support by cleansing the water element within our body. From blood to digestive juices, to interstitial fluids, our body is comprised primarily of water. If we are dehydrated or have limited access to clean water, our cells begin to struggle and work less than optimally. Shunite works to heal the crystalline matrix of water, providing healing and help to each system. This enhances overall wellness and our ability to go with the flow.

Because it is so coherent in its protective forces, this stone is ideal to wear throughout the day. Wake up, feel ready and refreshed with shungite as your ally.

Affirmation:

I am free from all unwanted energies. I can breathe.

7am

LEPIDOLITE

Feeling fresh and bright as a perfect summer morning, the energy of lepidolite drenches our essence in a sumptuous field of fresh love.

This stone, which comes in soft shades of lilac, purple, pink, and gray, is a reasonably priced combination of lithium, aluminum, and silicates and is found in deposits in North and South America and Africa. Because it contains lithium, a known mood stabilizer, this stone is chemically compounded to bring about emotional ease, peace, and a wonderful sense of calm. Lepidolite, a bestie stone, readily lends a steady hand.

Capable of working well with each of our chakras, lepidolite resonates most powerfully with the 4th and 6th energy centers. This specificity inspires us to see ourselves and others in the light of compassion and with the eyes of Love. Held safe in this vibration, we can more willingly forgive others and find peace within our heart. Then, as we release old feelings of resentment, our body detoxifies the stagnant emotions that lead to sluggish digestion, apathy, and "brain fog." This release promotes clarity, calm, and balance.

On the physical level, lepidolite proves a tonic for the nerves, may soothe symptoms of ADHD, and can help rewire the brain when insomnia persists. It may support electrolyte balance in the body.

With this spirit of peace fused in our heart and nestled in our mind, we can focus, concentrate, and set goals that are achieved each and every day. Not to mention, we learn to accept ourselves all along the way.

This day is yours!

Affirmation:

I find gentle ways to nurture myself through the day.

8am

FIRE AGATE

After opening the heart with lepidolite, fire agate primes our body and ignites our will.

Fire agate is a variety of banded chalcedony, part of the quartz family. This particular agate contains iron, which gives it a coppery-red flashy quality. Most commonly found in North America, this gem is a wonderful catalyst for enhancing positive physical experiences in life. Easy to find at a low cost, fire agate is a worthy ally.

Since it works specifically with the first three chakras, fire agate skillfully grounds and centers our energy, promotes feelings of calm, cool confidence, and gives a boost of creative juice. When we find this flow, the day takes shape in a way that feels engaging, enriching, and uplifting.

Bearing qualities of both the fire and earth elements, this gem aligns our will with our actions. With this synergistic connection, we have the desire to act and energy to move, making our thoughts manifest into our reality. Fire agate is a perfect catalyst for shifting procrastination, stagnation, or hesitation into courageous steps and bold deeds.

This stone also primes our digestive juices and can help boost metabolism. Fire agate can ease constipation and "nervous" bladder. Irregular menstrual cycles may be regulated and normalized and stalled labor may be pushed into high gear with this gem.

Pelvic, hip, and leg flexibility can be increased with consistent use of fire agate.

Fire agate helps us open to warm, intimate relationships where we can be truly known and deeply loved. In times of vulnerability, the vibration of this treasure harbors us safely from the storm.

A wonderful way to greet the new day—with an appetite whetted for life and a body that is ready to go.

From physical healing to creative expressions, fire agate will help us get the work done.

Affirmation:

I readily receive my good.

9am

SPINEL

Coming in a range of colors and originating in metamorphic and igneous rock, spinel offers our entire system a triumphant boost of the highest vibration.

Mined in Asia and Africa, this stone contains a variety of compounds that account for the diverse color palate. From aluminum, magnesium, iron, zinc, and nickel, spinel blends with numerous elements; likewise, it blends quite well with other crystals and stones. Spinel is affordable and accessible at most rock shops.

Perhaps you've heard the saying, "This is a new day!" or "Time for a fresh start." Yet, all too often, we slide back into the same old, same old, endlessly repeating patterns and habits, going through the motions because it's just what we do.

If you've felt stuck in a rut, spinel will shift this for you.

Because it works on each chakra, spinel infuses us with a sense of purpose, a spirit of hope, and a knowing that we can create our life in a way that supports our personal dreams and goals. With an ability to promote a sense of balanced optimism, spinel activates the realization that with patience and persistence, timing and trust, we can experience life inspired.

On the physical level, spinel may improve any joint, muscle, bone, or dental issues. Arthritis, carpal tunnel syndrome, TMJ, and prosthetic joints can benefit from ongoing use of this mineral.

This gem may assist in conditions of the spine. Back, rib, or hip pain may be decreased as flexibility and mobility is increased with spinel.

Spinel can guide us in choosing healthy, nourishing foods, and we enjoy a balanced appetite.

Based on the color, the stone you will work with will give an added boost to the charka corresponding in hue. For example, green spinel will first open the heart, then work to clear and amplify the rest of the energy field.

Light and lovely, steady and strong, spinel is a worthy ally in life.

Affirmation:

My clarity is replenished, and my strength restored as I draw from Source.

10am

KYANITE

The first time I laid eyes on kyanite I was mesmerized; it looks like a stone that comes from another world. Rippling, forming in wing-like chunks, this unique mineral is near the hardness of a diamond. Found in numerous colors and distributed worldwide, kyanite is affordable—lots of bang for the buck.

Containing aluminum and silicates, kyanite often neighbors with garnet, amethyst, and staurolite, so it works well with all varieties of quartz.

Kyanite quickly and precisely clears the energy field. Then, in a wonderful whoosh of power, it aligns us with our soul with the soul of the planet. Fully oriented with heaven and earth, we feel a deep sense of peace with the flow of life.

Kyanite works with our entire being, this stone enhances intuition and awareness of our inner world. With love and compassion, we step into an acceptance of our journey and embrace a willingness to let old wounds go. Compassion is the foundation, the fuel, for all healing work—without self-love we inadvertently perpetuate the past. Compassion suspends then releases what was so that new foundations can be laid. Kyanite catalyzes our ability to engage in this transformational process.

On the physical level, kyanite may improve circulation, ease foot and leg conditions, relieve head and neck aches and dental pains, and lessen digestive or menstrual cramps. It may also promote mental clarity and an ability to think helpful and hopeful thoughts. The color of kyanite will give an added boost to the corresponding chakra.

Because kyanite connects us with the vibrant spirit of Earth, using this stone reminds us to grow and explore. Nature teaches cycles and growth, seasons and change, and times to be still. If you feel out of sorts or lost in the mire, kyanite will place you gently on solid ground.

Affirmation:

I am a powerful presence for Spirit. I am balanced and free!

11am

SERPENTINE

Named because of its smooth, green appearance, serpentine is a magnesium containing mineral that is widely distributed and easily obtained.

Connected with earth and water, this stone helps us feel steady in our emotions, capable of attaining balance, and able to receive love. Thankfully, despite the name, no snakes need ever be involved!

First, serpentine gently opens and strengthens our connection to Mother Earth. As this happens, we experience a sense of belonging, a feeling of home. Holding serpentine to the heart sparks a remembrance within that we are woven into the Earth and connected to one another.

As this experience deepens, our energy expands and exceeds our previously held limits. So often we allow ourselves to be weighed down in the physical mire. Working with serpentine, we receive a clear infusion of uplifting energy that helps us remember we are spirits living a human life. With this sense of purpose and place, we relax more into the flow and trust the process.

Serpentine levels out the bumpy patches in our energy field and helps us feel whole, inspired, peaceful, and calm. This proves especially helpful when overcoming communication difficulties or physical challenges. We begin to "shed" the skin of old patterns and allow new, healthy choices to lead us.

On the physical level, serpentine may enhance our endurance, amplify results of exercise and athletic training, improve hand eye coordination, and spur a confident decisiveness. It can sharpen our vision and ease eye strain in times of prolonged study. For any spine or nerve issues, serpentine may ease aches and pains and promote flexibility. This stone also proves effective during meditation as a calming and centering ally.

The sweet nature of serpentine is suitable for kids and animals. When placed in a room, this stone will emit a peaceful energy that touches all.

Affirmation:

I release old patterns and enjoy this moment. The past limits me no more!

Noon

YELLOW TOPAZ

This bright and cheery crystal is a sweet drop of heaven on Earth.

Highly regarded since ancient times, topaz is a mineral bearing fluorine, aluminum, and silicon and is found distributed worldwide. Named for an island in the Mediterranean Sea, and the Sanskrit word meaning "fire," topaz comes in a variety of colors. Small samples of this beauty are priced reasonably.

Browsing the local crystal shop one bright Saturday, a sweet little thing caught my eye. Like a kid in a candy store, I hungrily smiled and got a closer look. Golden, warm, and filled with rainbow prisms, this crystal feels giddy, like walking on sunshine.

Topaz affects the first, third, and sixth chakras, grounding, empowering, pacifying the energy field. Deepening this kinship, topaz sparks our ability to tap into a strong will, a boundless spirit of optimism, and clear motivation to persist with confidence toward our goals. Topaz clears away the need to control or the demand for guarantees, and places us in the blessed assurance that we can attain the sweet life.

In times of heavy emotions, when feeling anxious or overwhelmed, yellow topaz helps spur us through the heavy so we can frolic in the light.

Topaz enhances meditation, slowing the annoying chatter that distracts us from deeper wisdom and higher vision. When feeling intuition is "out of reach" or "off," this gem nudges us back in the flow.

Physical benefits of this crystal include enhancing bone health, aiding digestion, and easing headaches from muscle strain.

Yellow topaz brightens life and sugars the day.

Affirmation:

I enjoy nourishing myself with good food, uplifting news, and positive relationships. I am well!

1pm

AMETRINE

Two crystals are better than one! Ametrine is a combination of amethyst and citrine that soothes and stimulates our energy in a powerful and wonderful way. Found in Brazil and at various locations in North America, this gem is relatively common and reasonably priced.

Citrine and amethyst work synergistically to bless and empower our energy field. First, amethyst centers and sooths the mind, clearing the aura of any toxic or fear-based energies. As this happens, waves of peace and feelings of expansion ensue. Next, citrine bolsters energy in the solar plexus, growing feelings of confidence, clarity, and purpose. This process of pacifying and empowering assists us as we express our wants and needs in a calm, cool fashion.

Ametrine may also assist us in recognizing and accepting abundance and financial prosperity. With the assured energy of this crystal, we believe in our worthiness and allow good to flow, and stay, in our lives.

Another powerful effect of ametrine is its knack for allowing us to have confidence in our ability to release old habits as we openly explore a new future. When we yearn for change, but feel obligated to tradition, this gem sets us in a space of openness where we can freely and curiously explore. This proves beneficial when leaving a relationship, a church, or a conventional practice. Ametrine elevates our energy so we can see all options as being equal and then choose from a place of love.

Physically, ametrine can relieve head and sinus pressure, bump up metabolism, and assist the liver with detoxification. Ametrine may also strengthen the endocrine system as it balances hormones and digestive enzymes.

As the afternoon begins, ametrine will lift you through the slump.

Affirmation:

Drawing from Spirit's energy, I shine my light in the world.

2pm
ZOISITE WITH RUBY

If there were a stone to give sunshine on a cloudy day, or when it's cold outside, and you want the month of May, zoisite with ruby is your girl.

This combination consists of a silicate mineral with ruby. Ranging in color from green to blue to gray to lilac, this delightful blend lavishes you with a comforting vibe to heed and a gentle light to follow through the afternoon. Zoisite alone can be found widely in Asia, Africa, and Australia, yet the coupled stone comes from India. This mineral is easily obtained and highly affordable.

Zoisite first lifts and lightens the entire energy filed like an open window to a stuffy room. Then, with extra love and care for the first, fourth, and sixth chakras, zoisite with ruby finds and expands our inner joy, infuses vitality, spurs growth, and casts us a glimpse of who we truly are. This optimism and open heartedness spurs us to receive more good in our world and to feel at ease with choices that bring to light the best of who we are.

On a physical level, zoisite with ruby can facilitate feelings of compassion that catalyze action steps to healing. For example, if you're feeling overwhelmed about starting yoga, but really know you need the stretch, ruby with zoisite can foster a sense of hopeful curiosity and a willingness to "just see" how it might work out.

This mineral can also help with muscle, bone, and joint imbalances as we learn how to exercise and nourish the structures that support our body lovingly and consistently. Zoisite with ruby may also promote relaxation in the head, neck, and shoulders, as it cools mental over-activity.

This mineral will bless you in the afternoon and keep you strong all day long.

Affirmation:

As I focus on my truth, I trust my soul to guide me.

3pm

KUNZITE

Pure love.

Kunzite is a lithium containing silicate crystal that comes in shades of pink, violet, and clear. Found in Pakistan, Afghanistan, Brazil, Madagascar, and California, this jewel resonates with all aspects of the Divine Heart. Reasonably easy to find at a moderate price, kunzite opens, heals, strengthens, and fills the heart with love.

In our culture, we tend to focus on performance and perfection, product and results. Kunzite gently awakens us to the spark of love in our neighbors, the waitress, the person at the intersection, the trees, and the strands of light that connect all of us in this world. Though we look and act differently, kunzite activates within us feelings of powerful and profound Divine love.

When working with kunzite, compassion, patience, and an appreciation for the goodness of life begin to emanate from our core. Holding this stone at the heart chakra promotes stillness, peace, and a profound sense of unconditional love.

As this crystal works coherently with the heart, it has the capacity to activate our wisdom. Wisdom is more than knowledge and intellect; wisdom is the spirit of understanding that comes from the soul. Accessing this timeless essence, we reconcile the past, embrace the present, and trust the future. Wisdom is the greater part of us that meets each moment with grace, ease, and Love.

On the physical level, this mineral may improve cardiovascular and respiratory function as well and balance thyroid and other hormonal conditions.

Kunzite's energy is soft at first, so consistently connecting with it offers ongoing and cumulative benefits.

When fear and doubt lurk, kunzite calmly and clearly reminds us that Love is our path, our nature, our power.

Affirmation:

I push away blocks and dispel all fear. I am worthy of love.

4pm

TANGERINE QUARTZ

Not too bold, never too mild, tangerine quartz is a sparkly little firecracker that ignites our desires in flashy fashion. This quartz variety gleans an orange hue from iron inclusions. Found in Brazil and Madagascar, tangerine quartz is reasonably priced and can be found at most specialty rock shops.

Clear quartz opens and energizes all our chakras. With the iron inclusions, our second chakra, the center of creativity, emotions, and sensuality receives an extra boost. Thanks to this enhancement, we readily tap into a sense of childlike enthusiasm and wonder that sets a space where curiosity, innocence, and joy pour forth from our cells and into the world when working with this treasure.

Similarly, tangerine quartz assists us in rousing our senses. Often, we are so rush, rush, rush, think, think, think, go, go, go that we forget our personal tastes and our zest for life. Apathy and ambivalence are symptoms of dulled senses. Tangerine quartz digs deep into our sacral chakra and excavates the power of zeal. Awakened sensual desires stimulate us to seek what we want and feel satisfied with just enough. This is particularly helpful when working through blocks, recovering from illness, or when struggling with dysthymia and depression.

Spiritually, tangerine quartz primes our body to feel the presence of our non-physical helpers. For example, when thinking of a loved one who has passed, we might experience chills or ringing in the ears. Tangerine quartz sensitizes our bodies to experience and recognize these wonderful validations.

Physically, tangerine quartz can calm the tummy and bring balance to the kidneys. It may also assist with bladder issues, constipation or irritable bowel, irregular menstrual cycles, and diverticulitis.

Tangerine quartz spurs our five senses and reminds us that life is a gift filled with good.

Affirmation:

My senses uplift and delight me. I savor the goodness of Light.

5pm

HEMATITE

Hematite is a mineral that derives its name from the Greek word for blood; when crushed into a powder it appears deep red. Containing iron, hematite is a potent tool for helping us settle into the physical world.

In its tumbled form, hematite appears dark black with a sheen of silver. This mineral is easily obtained and is widely distributed throughout the world.

Hematite works with our entire energy field to clear the clutter and dust off any extraneous, stray, or rogue energies that do not serve us. When we are cleared and freed from all the junk, hematite anchors us into the physical body by expanding and energizing the root chakra. As this happens, we feel calm, strong, and vital; aligned with the truth and ready to embody the best of who we are.

This grounded energy proves beneficial in many ways. First, when we are present and clear about who we are and what we want, we can manifest rapidly in the physical world. Additionally, if we have become too obsessed or overly enamored with body image or physical appearance, if we're judging ourselves harshly for not being "perfect" enough, hematite stimulates us to come into an appreciation of the body we have and the life we've been given. This mineral also helps us dispel the spaciness that can sometimes result from too much time spent in mental activity or with our head in the metaphysical clouds.

Hematite may enhance our ability to enter deeper states of meditation. With our physical body set, our spirit can wander and wonder far and wide without needless distraction. Prayers and meditation are amplified with this gem.

Often, we resist the physical or resent the challenges of life. Working with hematite releases us from those feelings and allows us to accept and celebrate the body we've been given, the path upon which we walk, and the ability to live a life we love.

Hematite works consistently, steadily, and readily. I find it a go to in times of stress and hardship.

Affirmation:

Knowing I am protected, I take inspired action to live my life.

6pm

MOSS AGATE

With its bands of brown, white, and fuzzy green, this mineral, part of the chalcedony family, offers powerful and coherent pulses of energy that help us center in our body and see the beauty of nature surrounding and supporting us. Widely distributed, moss agate is easy to acquire and can be found in large specimens at a reasonable cost.

The structure of moss agate resets our energy field and brings the truth of who we are to our immediate consciousness. Too often, the drama of life sweeps up our essence, snaring our thoughts and stealing our joy. Instead of denying, ignoring, or brushing challenges aside, moss agate brings strength, connectedness, and determination to the forefront.

With this resolve, we get busy living.

Imagine a tiller that churns the soil to bring fertile earth to the surface. In this fresh dark earth, seeds can be planted, and the barren land can be renewed. Moss agate works in similar fashion, resurfacing our joy and hope to the top, providing a space where we plant seeds for a bright future. Because moss agate opens the heart chakra with steady pulses of calming and nurturing energy, using this stone provides an assuredness that we can heal, release, and, with the support of positive forces around us, grow.

Focusing on the first, second, and heart charkas, this stone promotes bone health, hormonal balance, appetite regulation, and can improve cardiac function and circulation. It may be particularly helpful with musculoskeletal concerns in the chest and shoulders. Moss agate can inspire us to stand up straight, breathe deep, and move with life.

For those interested in gardening, flowers, essential oils, medicinal herbs, and natural forms of healing, moss agate primes our spirit to connect with the wisdom of Mother Nature. We learn to hug, listen, and talk with the trees.

Moss agate is a humble, unassuming, steady stone.

Affirmation:

My soul is refreshed as I see beauty around me. I feel blessed.

7pm

MALACHITE

If there were a mineral that could provide a cloak of invisibility, malachite would fit to a tee. A mesmerizing stone, swirling green and blue with layers rippling all around, this gem gleans its color from inclusions of copper. Revered for its beauty and respected for its mystical aura, malachite use dates to antiquity. A prized stone, malachite has adorned high ranking society from Egypt, Greece, Rome, Europe, Israel, and Russia. Sourced from Australia, Africa, and North and South America, this gem comes at a low cost and is easy to find.

Malachite works powerfully with the 3rd and 4th chakras. After attuning to our energy field, this little drop of magic begins to push out negativity and thwart low vibrations that might be lurking on the side. Next, it ramps up the aura with confidence and assuredness that exudes a spirit of invulnerability and extends a message of strong defense. As incoming negativity senses this power, it buzzes off!

Malachite calibrates us to the power of love and the strength within the heart. In our culture, intuition, emotions, and desires are quickly dismissed or actively suppressed in favor of intellect, conformity and productivity. We are trained to live according to society's needs rather than our soul's desires. With malachite, we feel confident enough to listen to our inner wisdom, forge a new path, and let go of the thoughts and opinions of others.

This stone is perfect for starting new projects, changing directions, or letting go of the tendency to "caretake" others.

Physically, malachite strengths digestion, helps with kidney health and fluid balance, resets our metabolism, and keeps the heart and circulatory system strong. Malachite can also soothe the adrenals so that we don't fall prey to "flight or fight" reactions. This lovely may ease sore throats and soften muscles of the cervical spine and neck.

Importantly, this stone inspires us to speak from the heart.

As we awaken to truth, strip away any illusion, malachite proves an invaluable tool.

Affirmation:

My heart is open to give and receive love.

8pm

CHALCEDONY

Harvested and prized in Ancient Greece, Egypt, and Rome, chalcedony is a quartz-based mineral that comes in various colors based on local mineral inclusions. Light and lovely, chalcedony comes from mines worldwide and is easily obtained at an affordable price. Colors range from purple to blue to white, with occasional reds and oranges, too.

Chalcedony is the stone of peace and grace. Like a fuzzy blanket in winter, or soft serve ice cream in summer, chalcedony comforts our energy field and casts a supple, warm glow on our inner world. When we feel this emotional balance, new, more supportive ideas, insights, and feelings emerge. Under its lovely spell, we learn to release worry, undo insecurity, and listen to our inner wisdom.

The purple variety of chalcedony strengthens our feelings of harmony and unity with the world. Working with this stone, we readily recognize our connection with a Greater Power and find peace with our place in the Divine Plan.

Because it contains quartz, chalcedony offers purification, balance, and cleansing of the entire energy field. The blues can open and soothe the throat, our 5th chakra, and purples can ease a tired or strained head by balancing the crown, 7th chakra.

On the physical level, this stone may boost the immune system, enhance thyroid function, foster healthy fluid balance, and ease respiratory conditions. Chalcedony may be of benefit in dealing with motion sickness, dizziness, or vertigo. It may soften and shift TMJ and neurologic conditions that affect the face, head, or neck. This treasure may ease eye aches and strains and provide relief for head pains.

Continued and ongoing appreciation of chalcedony will amplify our ability to attract and manifest people and situations that reflect our highest good.

Chalcedony eases the mind and buoys the heart, allowing our entire essence to feel love.

Affirmation:

I am relaxed and receptive, centered, and serene.

9pm
TURQUOISE

The traditional birthstone for December, turquoise is an easily obtainable gemstone that contains copper, aluminum, and hydrous phosphate. Like a deep, tropical blue sea, this stone blisses our energy field with serenity, positivity, purification, wisdom, and love. Turquoise can be found in shades of white, purple, and yellow, though much less frequently.

Mined in the Middle East, Australia, Asia, and North America, this treasure comes at a range of price points and is easy to come by.

Resonating with the heart, throat, and 3rd eye chakra, this mineral expands our sense of self-love and worthiness. To accomplish this, turquoise rids our energy of negativity from within and bounces out lower energies from our environment so that we feel free to be who we are. In this genuine spirit of self-acceptance and love, we let go of old relationships, friendships, work patterns, spiritual beliefs, or destructive patterns that have kept love at bay.

Turquoise helps foster within us the courage to try new ideas, to test out new patterns, and to give ourselves permission to fly. Inspiring curiosity and exuberance, turquoise obliterates perfectionism and erects our connection to what lifts us high.

Physically, this stone may help heal throat, heart, lung, shoulder, and neck issues. Inner and middle ear issues may be cleared with turquoise's loving vibe.

Sinus, jaw, and swallowing imbalances may be lessened, too.

The ancient Egyptians reached for turquoise to help with meditation and to ease joint issues such as rheumatism. The Zuni people of America believed turquoise would bring luck, health, and good journeys; the Aztecs considered it a stone of love; only royalty could wear clothes of this color.

Mentally, turquoise reminds us of our worth and helps us feel a deeper sense of pride in who we are. From here, we carry ourselves with dignity and poise.

With its noble air and powerful presence, proves a perfect pillow partner as you prepare for bed.

Affirmation:

My heart-felt intentions are received and returned with love.

10pm

SNOWFLAKE OBSIDIAN

Like gazing into a flurried globe at Christmas time, this mineral is a lovely blend of glass and volcanic debris that induces feelings of peace, tranquility, and stillness. Black bedecked with little bursts of flurry looking inclusions, snowflake obsidian is widely distributed and can be obtained at a reasonable cost.

This stone, which aligns with the 1st and 6th chakras, has a strong energy that fosters insight, optimism, wisdom, and a willingness to see the light even in dark times. These feelings are enhanced by snowflake obsidian's ability to clear negativity from the root chakra, releasing any fears or imbalances that may have arisen during the day, and settling our bodies back into our innate rhythm as we prepare for sleep time. Then, we release and make peace with the day that is done.

Completing this, snowflake obsidian next readies the mind to connect with higher wisdom and guidance during dreamtime. As we rest, our intuition is primed and opened to communicate and illuminate our highest good. Be it past life recall, seeing our angels, or understanding a solution to a difficult problem, this treasure aligns our energy field, so these connections become fluid, effortlessly attained.

Physical benefits of this gem may include improved digestion, strengthened kidney functions, release of jaw pain or dental issues, and cooling of frazzled or overexcited nerves. Snowflake obsidian proves an invaluable ally when changing habits, especially those involving food.

A beauty to behold, snowflake obsidian is a perfect stone to tuck under your pillow at night. Magic, optimism, and clarity will greet you.

Affirmation:

I clear away the mental clutter and let my body and soul merge with Spirit.

11pm

LABRADORITE

Known in the Inuit traditions as the stone of frozen fire, labradorite was believed by ancients to be the Northern Lights captured in crystalized form. Dashing and bold, this blazing beauty flashes dazzling blues and greens as it catches and reflects the light. Bearing calcium, sodium, silica, and oxygen, this treasure in mined from North America and northern Europe and is easily obtained in a wide range of price points.

Labradorite offers a wondrous array of benefits: first, it stabilizes our aura and then releases blocks. Next, of fortifies and brings extra layers of protection as it prepares our mind to begin deeper inner work. After this is complete, labradorite opens our intuition and accesses our subconscious mind so that we can see the unrecognized beliefs, patterns, or thought forms that hold us back. When this happens, we have the opportunity to release, change, and choose from the best divine possibilities.

If your mental activity kicks up with the lights go down, labradorite assists in clearing and calming restless and random thoughts so that we readily tune to our wisdom. Because our dream time can serve as a stage for insight and inspiration, this stone gives charge to imagination and creative problem-solving skills while amplifying our ability to recall nighttime revelations.

Physically, this stone benefits the blood, bones, and nerves. For conditions such as sinus pressure, TMJ, and eye strain, labradorite may prove beneficial.

As our body and mind are settled and relaxed, we are ready for a restful night's sleep. This stone is a wonderful comforter, protector, and healer.

Affirmation:

I relax into this moment and let my inner vision awaken. I see love.

Midnight
PETALITE

With its striking resemblance to quartz, this dazzling beauty is more difficult to come by but well worth the price. Color varieties include clear, white, and pale pink. Found in Brazil and a few countries of Africa, petalite comes at a decent price.

Petalite yields a coherent energy that lifts our minds into the highest places. Often, we get stuck in trauma and anxiety, or languish in our memories, issues, and old stories. Fears, worst case scenarios, and an endless stream of "what ifs?" may barrage us as we lay down at night. Sleeping with petalite affords us an opportunity to access new and vibrant places in the mind that are untouched by the ego's prattle. Once we are open to these fresh and fertile energies, we have an opportunity to see and know who we truly are in Spirit's eyes.

This proves beneficial during phases of life when we feel stuck. Though routines may provide a sense of stability, often monotony can lead to heaviness and a sense of powerlessness. We may yearn for a change but believe it impossible. We may want a shift but cannot conceive how situations could differ. Petalite pulls back the curtains in our creative mind and shows us a new truth.

If you are drawn to the angelic realm, petalite will deftly direct you to Heaven's messengers as you open more fully to guardians, spirit helpers, totem animals, and guides.

On the physical level, this gem may assist our core functions—motor skills, respiration, sleep cycles, hormonal regulation, physical balance, and overall brain function. It may ease post-partum adjustments, promote recovery from surgery, and prove beneficial when sleeping in a new place. Petalite is wonderful in supporting us in transition: puberty, menopause, birth, grief, and other life changes.

The soft, soothing energy of petalite proves advantageous for those struggling with anxiety, ADHD, or hypertension. As it can have a very powerful vibration, this stone is generally not recommended for children.

When we rise to the place where stillness prevails, our body, mind, and soul remember that all is well.

Affirmation:

My heart and mind are clear of anything but Love.

1am

SODALITE

Deepest of blues spangled with coppers and whites, sodalite is a sodium bearing crystal found widely distributed throughout North and South America. Though typically inky blue, this beauty sometimes occurs in white, gray, or yellowish colors and is easy to find at an affordable price in most rock shops.

Sodalite is a stone of deep and quiet contemplation. Stillness, calm, and a palpable spirit of peace radiate outward in bands from sodalite into our energy field. Like waves of the ocean, ebb and flow, rise and fall, in and out, sodalite's energy waltzes into our imagination, our sixth chakra, inspiring genius and innovation of thought.

This stone is perfect for quickening intuitive abilities and enhancing dream recall. Lucid and prophetic nighttime journeys may occur with ongoing use. Because this stone is so calming, placing one under the pillow will ease insomnia and sooth a troubled mind.

When faced with stormy circumstances or shifting sands, sodalite proves a wonderful ally. If you tend to overthink or overanalyze, if your self-confidence relies more on the reactions of others, sodalite can spark within you a memory of your inherent self-worth.

For the physical body, sodalite may clear sinus issues, alleviate mouth, or head pain, and promote an overall relaxation response. Sodalite can help with electrolyte and fluid balance, and well as assisting the pituitary gland with appropriate hormone release and regulation. Sodalite may also assist with hair growth or catalyze regrowth in times of loss.

Sodalite remains one of my most prized and favorite "go to" crystals.

Endless wonders await within when we work with sodalite.

Affirmation:

My inner wisdom speaks to me in dreams and signs that I recognize.

2am

APATITE

What a gift to work with apatite.

This stone is a combination of two to three different calcium containing minerals and can be found in a wide assortment of colors: blue, gray, white, yellow, green, purple, light red, and brown. Easy to acquire and native to Mexico, Canada, Germany, and parts of Russia, this stone works seamlessly on many different layers of our body and energy field.

As we sleep, our physical structures undergo tremendous vital, restorative, and regenerative processes. From recycling old blood cells, building new hormones, balancing metabolism, and strengthening teeth and bones, the physical complement of our spiritual essence blisses with a nightly make-over. Apatite, like a super food of the crystal world, facilitates and promotes our body's efforts toward wellness. Additionally, apatite boosts the immune system and helps restore the normal flora of the gut.

As the name may suggest, apatite stimulates us to crave healthy and healing sustenance. Food is medicine, and apatite will prescribe what is right for the body, mind, and soul. Off the plate, apatite whets our taste for healthy and balanced relationships.

Spiritually, apatite amplifies our creativity and seeds inspiration by synchronizing our intuition with intellect, the chakras, and our meridians as it integrates the masculine and feminine aspects of who we are. From this state, as we rise for the day, we feel clear and ready to manifest good.

This gem may deepen our spirit of compassion toward ourselves and others. When we feel open-hearted and confident, we are ready to see good in the world.

Apatite allows us to appreciate and experience wonders.

Affirmation:

I access higher realms as my inner vison opens wide. I am connected.

3am

CHRYSOCOLLA

With a color palate that ranges from soft blue to vibrant turquoise to deep green, this copper, azurite, and malachite compounded mineral is found in Africa, South America, and the US. Reasonably priced, this natural beauty works in raw and polished form. Derived from Greek, the name means "gold glue." One peek at chrysocolla reveals veins of golden blending and binding other minerals to create something beautiful.

Though soft and gentle, chrysocolla packs a punch. As we sleep, our body begins the process of detoxification, healing, balancing, and replenishing bone, muscle, blood cells, liver and digestive cells, hormones, and neurotransmitters. Chrysocolla facilitates each of these processes. This lovely also soothes the mind and elevates our intuition during sleep time.

Additionally, chrysocolla helps ease heart ache and disappointment while sponging out self-judgement and guilt. Sweetly, this little stone reminds us to nurture ourselves and tend lovingly to that which gives us joy.

On a physical level, this stone may ease cramps, restless legs, and clear up night sweats. In addition, it can boost the lymphatic system, soften muscles of the neck and shoulders, and open the air passages.

Chrysocolla graciously teaches us to trust, receive, heal, and believe. We are unique creations forged by a loving creator.

So much good to be had from one sweet stone.

The spirit of grace fills me as I gently release uncertainty. I am peaceful and serene.

4am

OPAL

For some reason, I hesitated to connect with opal in the formative phases of my quest to embrace all things crystal. Looking back, I suspect that I somehow considered myself "unworthy" of opal, or that opal was reserved only for spiritual royalty—famous metaphysical authors, high priests, moon goddesses and the like. Sounds silly, but that limiting belief kept me from one on the sweetest, most powerful allies from the mineral kingdom.

The name opal comes from several traditions, as it has been revered and treasured by cultures all around the world for centuries. In Sanskrit, this mineral is called "upala" and means *precious stone.* The Greek word "opallius," meaning *change in color* was assigned to this stone.

Interestingly, opal has no set structure; in mineralogic terms it is classified as an "amorphous mineraloid." This anomaly of opal causes flashes, shines, and reflections of light cast beautifully and uniquely for each stone.

Distributed worldwide in many color varieties, opal is generally placed in two categories: precious and common. The color of the opal gives an indication as to what chakra is specifically energies; yet all opals offer wonderful, universal benefits.

Opal sooths and stabilizes our energy field and repairs and heals any cracks, tears, or old wounds in our aura. Next, it sets about reflecting light into our creative centers, our heart, and our mind. This infusion will counter depression and help catalyze us past stuck energy that stubbornly clings. Additionally, it sparks renewed connection to Mother Earth and awakens our awareness of how powerful and beautiful our Earth is.

Opal helps promote healthy kidney function and water balance, as well as benefitting the hair, skin, nails, and eyes. With strong kidney function, our immune system tasks well and our overall mental, physical, and emotional emanates vitality.

Peaceful, beautiful, accessible, opal is a wonderful companion for your spiritual life.

Affirmation:

I rest in harmony with my heart, soul, and Mother Earth. I am safe and loved.

5am
FELDSPAR

This hard working, always reliable, easy to find mineral is a wonderful transition stone between sleep and wake time. Taken from the German term "feld" meaning *field* and "spar" a mineralogic term for a stone with good cleavage, this little nugget is a combination of aluminum, calcium, potassium, and sodium. Widely distributed, feldspar constitutes 60% of Earth's crust and is found in a variety of colors. Feldspar, easy to carve, comes in a variety of sculpted fetishes—from little mushrooms to hefty flames. Highly affordable, this mineral is a trusty ally.

Feldspar's potency is matched by its gentle effect on our entire being.

Deepening the effects of chrysocolla, feldspar first sets about to straighten and align the chakras, meridians, and aura so that we think, feel, act, and function coherently. Next, it nurtures and deepens our sense of self-confidence and self-acceptance. This vital work helps us stay present, cut ties with the limits of the past, and access new visions, perspectives, and innovations within our heart and soul.

Feldspar also assists us setting goals and noticing synchronicities that support accomplishment. This mineral nudges us to be in the "right place at the right time" and, because of this, is often considered to bring luck and prosperity.

Physical benefits of feldspar may include relief of bone and joint pain or injury, clearing of irritated skin, ease from tooth pain, improved hair and nail growth, and a boost to the immune system. For swelling and areas where scar tissue is present, feldspar may reduce inflammation, and prompt muscle, skin, and tissue growth.

Boosting endurance, feelings of wakefulness, and a sense of being at "home" in the body, feldspar is truly a gift to have in any collection.

Affirmation:

My body, mind, and spirit are aligned for my good.

So here we are. We've rocked. We've rolled. We've managed to make it through every hour of each day with a crystal friend in tow.

And this is just the beginning.

My heart's desire is for you to go deeper, to explore beyond the covers of this book. Each day I discover a new geological treasure; my work with stones will inevitably be a lifelong love affair. Some rock my world; others sink…like a stone. Yet I value each encounter I have with my mineral friends. I love them, and I trust they love me.

Some days I wake up and tell myself, "You have to stop this crystal thing. No more!" I close my wallet and resolve to straighten up.

But then temptation, passion, curiosity sweeps my soul, taking hold. Thus, my collection grows.

I've come to accept this about myself. Character flaw, obsession, shortcoming, fascination. Call it what you like. It's how I rock…around the clock.

With love and blessings always to you,
Steff

PEBBLES ON THE PATH

Just for fun, I want to share a few of my personal go-to crystal combinations that I find potent, perky, and positively wonderful in getting specific jobs done.

Self-Confidence Charger
Libyan Desert Glass
Lemurian Quartz
Citrine
Amethyst

Get My Engines Running
Moldavite
Brucite
Iolite

Ego Party Crasher
Alexandrite
Labradorite
Rose Quartz
Agni Manitite

To See Infinity and Beyond
Moldavite
Phenacite
Lapis Lazuli

Manifesting Fast as a Flash
Fulgurite
Green Jade
Silver Sheen Obsidian

Getting My Energy Ducks in a Row
Serpentine
Wavellite
Blue Tiger's Eye
Angelite

My Energy Dust Buster
Pink Amethyst
Orca Agate
Mahogany Obsidian
Tibetan Tektite

Talking with the Dead
Hemimorphite
Scolecite
Larimar
Stone of Israel

Opening My Mind to New Dimensions
Astrophylite
Apophylite
Moldavite

To Talk to the Dog
Jade
Pyrite
Crazy Lace Agate
Charoite

FOR FURTHER READING

The Crystal Bible by Judy Hall
The Book of Stones by Robert Simmons
The Complete Crystal Handbook by Cassandra Eason
Crystals: The Modern Guide to Crystal Healing by Julia Van Doren

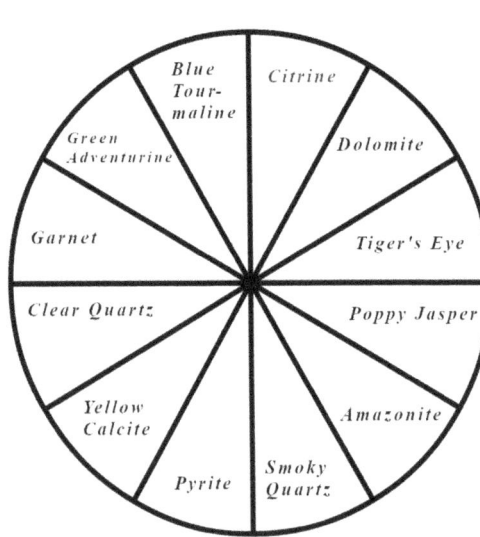

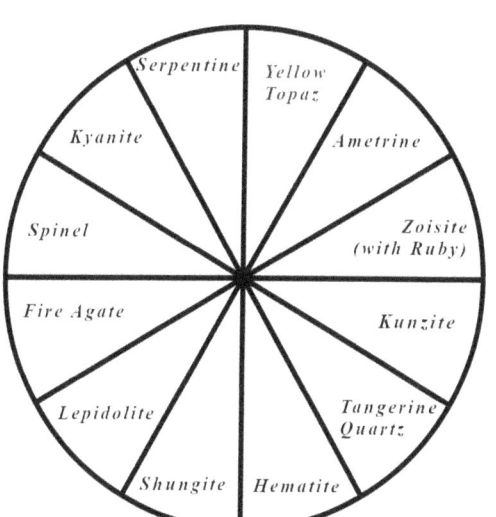

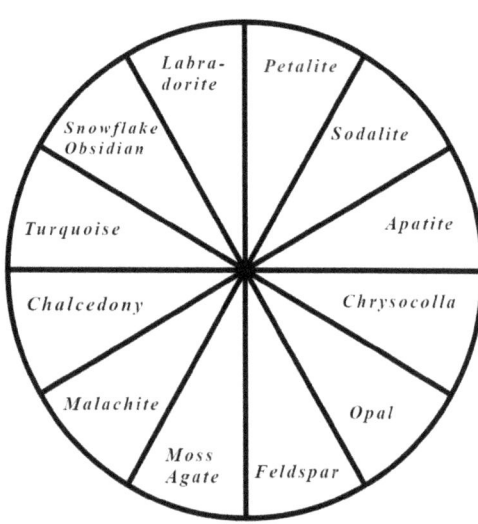

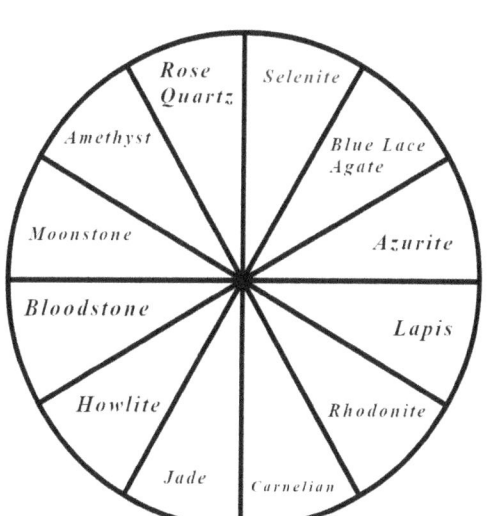

ABOUT THE AUTHOR

Steff (yes, she prefers Steff) Barton, RN is a devoted spiritual student and teacher. She works as a clairvoyant medium, Reiki healer, inspirational speaker, and desires to be a friend to all of life.

Her mission is to bring to light the unseen wisdom of spirit, the incredible presence of angels and spirit helpers, and the truth of each person's divinity. She offers private consultations, group sessions, and crystal healings.

Please visit her website **www.angelsinsight.com** to learn more about her work and her vision. She can also be found on social media

Facebook: Angels InSight
Twitter: @Steffany Barton
IG: steffanybarton

www.ingramcontent.com/pod-product-compliance
Lightning Source LLC
LaVergne TN
LVHW051219070526
838200LV00064B/4964